IMAGES
of America

MUSCATINE

PETER MUSSER AND LAURA MUSSER McCOLM, 1910. Lumber baron Peter Musser built a home at 1314 Mulberry Avenue for his daughter Laura Musser McColm in 1908. After Laura died in 1964, her heirs, stepdaughter Mary Catherine McWhirter and niece Mary Musser Gilmore, donated the home and grounds to the city to establish an art gallery and museum in Laura's memory. (Courtesy of Muscatine Art Center.)

ON THE COVER: Ladies from the 1910 theatrical production *Parada* pose with parasols. Muscatine Art Center records identify the women, in no particular order, as Sade McQuesten, Emma Bielefeld, Gertrude Bersch Christopherson, Julia Fuller Fagan, Lib Koetting, Myrel Nesper Southall, Anna Knoll Korte, Grace Griffen, and Ms. Higgins. (Courtesy of Muscatine Art Center.)

IMAGES
of America

MUSCATINE

Kristin McHugh-Johnston

ARCADIA
PUBLISHING

Published by Arcadia Publishing
Charleston, South Carolina

Library of Congress Control Number: 2010929512

For all general information, please contact Arcadia Publishing:
Telephone 843-853-2070
Fax 843-853-0044
E-mail sales@arcadiapublishing.com
For customer service and orders:
Toll-Free 1-888-313-2665

Visit us on the Internet at www.arcadiapublishing.com

Dedicated to all who passionately preserve the past for future generations

CONTENTS

ACKNOWLEDGMENTS

When Irving Richman set out to compile Muscatine's history in 1911, he needed two volumes to capture the highlights and to record the biographies of local residents who made profound contributions to the community. Today it would take at least a dozen books to document Muscatine's awe-inspiring entrepreneurial spirit.

Muscatine in the Images of America Series was never intended to be a complete history of the community that has been my home since 1995. It is merely a snapshot of those who laid the foundation of Muscatine's first 100 years.

This work is the culmination of months of combing through the archives and history files of the Muscatine Art Center and the Musser Public Library. Thank you to art center director Barbara Christensen and library director Pam Collins for opening your archives and graciously dedicating staff to assist me with the gathering of information. I am deeply indebted to Muscatine Art Center registrar Virginia Cooper and Musser Public Library photograph archivist Sheila Chaudoin. Virginia's patience and ability to recall the precise location of an artifact in the art center's archives is amazing. Sheila's dedication to preserving Oscar Grossheim's historic images of Muscatine is humbling.

Thank you to the many individuals and organizations that provided images, research, and fact checking: Lynn Bartenhagen, Keith Porter, assistant fire chief Mike Hartman, police lieutenant Kevin Sink, Dan Clark, Kent Sissel, Tom Savage, Gary Weiskamp, Kathy Dantz, Bill Lindsay, Max Churchill, Melanie Alexander, the Kenneth Kemper family, Jennifer Blair, and the dedicated members of the Muscatine County Genealogy Society.

Thanks also to those who meticulously gathered, documented, and published local history before me, including Josiah P. Walton, John Mahin, Irving Richmond, William Randall, Douglas Randleman, Jon Carlson, and Jan Drum. I am also grateful to the organizations actively engaged in preserving Muscatine history, including the Muscatine Art Center's board of trustees, the Musser Public Library's board of trustees, and the Historic Muscatine, Inc., board of directors.

I also wish to thank Ted Gerstle, my Arcadia editor, for his expert guidance and insight. Finally, I extend my heartfelt gratitude to my husband, Eugene, who provided endless support and encouragement.

INTRODUCTION

Zebulon Pike was unsuccessful in his search for the source of the great Mississippi River during his exploration in 1805. He did, however, make note of the "Grindstone Bluffs" along a great east–west bend in the river. The Black Hawk Purchase in 1832 paved the way for pioneers to fan across the Mississippi River into the American Indian lands of Eastern Iowa.

The city of Muscatine can trace its beginning to a small trading post built to service passing steamships in 1833. Three years later, early land claims were mapped and a town named Bloomington emerged beneath the river bluffs. Soon flour and sawmills were established to meet the aspiring demand of new settlers. By 1839, Bloomington was incorporated and serving as the seat of government for Muscatine County. Iowa gained statehood in 1846, and three years later the name Bloomington was retired in favor of Muscatine.

Logs harvested from nearby forests, and later the lush lands of Wisconsin and Minnesota, supplied a seemingly endless stream of lumber for local mills. Muscatine was an important lumber city in the United States by the mid-1860s. In 1865, more than 13 million feet of lumber, six million shingles, and four million laths were shipped by rail or river. Entrepreneurs named Hershey, Musser, Huttig, Roach, Stein, and others amassed fortunes and generously gave time and money to city projects and organizations.

The arrival of railroads in 1855 expanded possibilities and spurred businessmen and city leaders to continually modernize the community with utilities, public transportation, and a bridge spanning the Mississippi River.

The sandy soil of the Muscatine Island made the land ideal for growing melon, fruit, and vegetables. Enterprise and railroad expansion allowed growers to spread the island's agricultural bounty regionally. Muscatine's H. J. Heinz canning facility, the first built outside of Pittsburgh, took advantage of the area's produce production.

The lumber industry was well established when John Frederick Boepple discovered that the thick mussels found in the Mississippi River were ideal for manufacturing mother-of-pearl buttons. Boepple launched his button company in 1891, and within a decade Muscatine was the undisputed "Pearl Button Capital of the World."

By 1905, Muscatine County's population swelled to over 28,000 on the heels of the lumber, button, and agricultural industries. From corner grocery stores to local factories, Muscatine's business districts produced or imported goods and materials for the growing community. Some ventures like the Thompson Motor Corporation were ambitious but short-lived. Several other companies, including the Muscatine Oat Meal Company and Barry Manufacturing, distributed items nationally. Others, such as the Kautz Bakery, Wilson's Shoe Store, the McColm Dry Good Company, and Batterson's, gave devoted service to Muscatine for generations.

Business and industry defined Muscatine's first 100 years, but a wealth of cultural spirit blossomed beyond the factories and fields. Benevolent families generously donated acres of land for city parks, music and theaters entertained the masses, and spiritual events and revivals energized the faithful.

Muscatine also produced scores of influential residents during this time. Entrepreneurs transformed the local economy, generously invested in the community, and all helped to define Muscatine's unique story. Samuel Clemens spent but a few months in Muscatine, but writing as Mark Twain he later recalled Muscatine's beautiful sunsets. Norman Baker gained fame in vaudeville and returned to Muscatine to pioneer local radio. Along the way, he crafted a merchandising empire and developed what he incredulously claimed was a cure for cancer. Civil rights pioneer Alexander Clark Sr. played a vital role in desegregating Iowa schools decades before the landmark *Brown vs. Board of Education* ruling.

The story of Muscatine traced through the following images provides just a snapshot of the pioneering men and women who left a legacy of innovation and work ethic that continues to define the community well into the 21st century.

One

HUMBLE BEGINNINGS

GREAT MUSCADINE PRAIRIE JOWA BY HENRY LEWIS, C. 1850. The city of Muscatine can trace its beginning to a small trading post in 1833. The post, financed by Col. George Davenport, was located near where the Mississippi River intersects Iowa Avenue. Historians through the years credit a man named Farnam for manning the post, although the first name of the early trader is not well documented. (Courtesy of Muscatine Art Center.)

MUSCADINE, JOWA, BY HENRY LEWIS, C. 1850. James Casey is widely recognized by historians as the first permanent resident within present-day Muscatine. Just downriver from Davenport's trading post, Casey (sometimes spelled Kasey) began operating a supply and fueling operation for passing riverboats in 1835. His business has also been documented as "Casey's Landing," and "Casey's Woodpile." Casey died in 1836 and is the first known white man to be buried within Muscatine city limits. Casey was first interred near present-day Seventh and Orange Streets, but his remains were later moved to Greenwood Cemetery. Today a large boulder located on Muscatine's renovated riverfront symbolically marks the location of Casey's Woodpile. This Henry Lewis lithograph, along with the one on the previous page, was originally titled and printed in Germany. (Courtesy of Muscatine Art Center.)

SKETCH OF THE PUBLIC SURVEYS IN THE IOWA TERRITORY, C. 1840. John Vanater (also spelled in historical references as Vanatta and Vanata) is credited by some as being the founder of what is today Muscatine. He purchased Colonel Davenport's land claim in 1836, quickly mapped the ground, and named the town Bloomington. (Courtesy of Muscatine Art Center.)

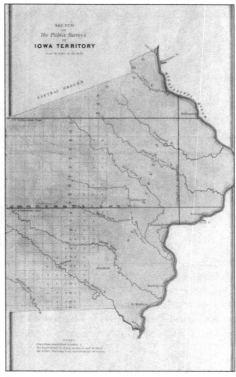

PINE CREEK GRIST MILL, 1937. Benjamin Nye, regarded as Muscatine County's first settler, founded Montpelier near Pine Creek in 1834. As demand for lumber grew with each new settler, Nye built a sawmill in 1835. A small gristmill was soon added and was replaced with the Pine Creek Grist Mill in 1848. This mill is now part of Wildcat Den State Park. (Courtesy of Musser Public Library.)

MISSISSIPPI RIVER MUSKATEEN PRAIRIE NOTEBOOK DRAWING BY CAPT. SETH EASTMAN, 1848. On December 7, 1836, the Wisconsin Territorial Legislature established Muscatine County under the name "Musquitine." The same legislative body further defined the county's borders under the name "Muscatine" in 1838. The town of Bloomington (now Muscatine) was named the county seat. (Courtesy of Muscatine Art Center.)

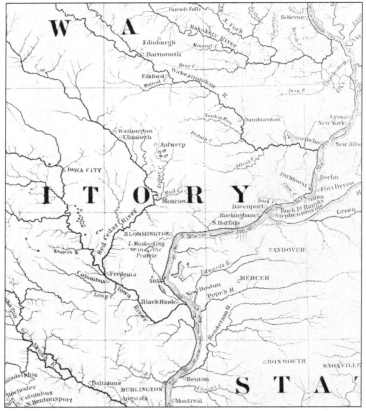

MAP OF THE HYDROGRAPHIC BASIN OF THE UPPER MISSISSIPPI RIVER, 1841. Three miles away, in present-day Sweetland Township, Dr. Eli Reynolds established the short-lived village of Geneva. Dr. Reynolds served as the local representative to the Wisconsin Territorial Legislature. In 1837, he petitioned the legislature to move the county seat from Bloomington to Geneva, but Territorial Governor Henry Dodge vetoed the measure. (Courtesy of Muscatine Art Center.)

PENNSYLVANIA HOUSE HOTEL, C. 1865. Some credit The Iowa House hotel, established in 1836 near Water (Mississippi Drive) and Chestnut Streets, as being the first wood frame building in present-day Muscatine. The establishment was bought by John G. Stein in 1847 and renamed Stein's Hotel. The name later changed to Pennsylvania House and continued operating as a hotel until it was torn down in 1880. (Courtesy of Musser Public Library.)

MUSCATINE LUMBER DISTRICT, 1901. A. O. and David Warfield built a water-powered mill along Mad Creek in 1838. It was the first sawmill within present-day Muscatine city limits. Five years later, Charles Cadle established the city's first steam-powered sawmill on Front Street (Mississippi Drive) near Oak Street. Lumber fueled Muscatine's prosperity in the latter half of the 1800s. (Courtesy of Muscatine Art Center.)

BLOOMINGTON BY JOHN CASPAR WILD, 1845. Bloomington was incorporated in February 1839 with a population of 71 and a total of 33 buildings. Within months, local leaders were elected. Joseph Williams was named president and Arthur Washburn, B. P. Howland, and Henry Reese served as trustees. One year later year, the population exceeded 500. Bloomington boasted 911 residents by 1844. (Courtesy of Muscatine Art Center.)

BENNETT'S MILL, C. 1866. Joseph Bennett opened a flour mill in a newly completed brick building along present-day West Mississippi Drive by 1849. A fire forced Bennett to rebuild a duplicate structure two years later. The mill produced flour until the 1870s. The building, portions of which remain standing, has housed a number of businesses, including the Muscatine Oat Meal Company and a button factory. (Courtesy of Muscatine Art Center.)

MUSCATINE POSTCARD, C. 1920. Often confused with towns of the same name in surrounding states, residents unsuccessfully petitioned to change Bloomington's name in 1842. A later attempt was successful, and in 1849 Bloomington ceased to exist in name and the town of Muscatine was born. The origin of the word "Muscatine" is disputed, although most believe it was derived from the language of the Mascoutin Indian tribe. (Courtesy of Muscatine Art Center.)

CITY OF MUSCATINE CHARTER, 1851. Muscatine was officially chartered in February 1851 and Zephaniah Washburn served as the city's first mayor. Local residents topped 2,500. The first bank, Green and Stone, opened the same year on Second Street. By 1856, the city council chambers were located above the bank. (Courtesy of Muscatine Art Center.)

Two

THE MIGHTY MISSISSIPPI

MISSISSIPPI RIVER VIEW FROM CHERRY STREET, C. 1900. Muscatine is situated along one of the largest east–west bends of the Mississippi River. The muddy waters greatly contributed to the city's transformation from a territorial trading post to an Iowa community rich in agricultural bounty and manufacturing ingenuity. In this image, Abraham Smalley's house on Second Street and the McKee Button Company overlook the mighty Mississippi. (Courtesy of Musser Public Library.)

DRURY'S LANDING, 1866. Drury's Landing, Illinois, benefitted greatly from Muscatine's growing needs. Located a few miles east upriver, Drury's Landing served as a hub where boats and ferries from the Iowa side of the river docked to trade goods. By the 1860s, its importance rapidly faded with the expansion of railroad transportation, and a permanent community was never established. (Courtesy of Musser Public Library.)

THE APEX FERRY, SKETCH BY JOHN MCGREER, C. 1850. Andrew Fimple and Giles Pettibone operated the Apex. Horses powered the ferry's two paddle wheels by walking on a footpath mechanism, but hauling capacity was limited. The *Muscatine* inaugurated steam-powered service in 1855 and other steam ferryboats followed. Ferry service fell by the wayside as land transportation improved and railroad service expanded. (Courtesy of Musser Public Library.)

TRANSPORTATION ON THE MISSISSIPPI RIVER AT MUSCATINE, C. 1900. For centuries, the Mississippi River has served as a transportation highway for people and goods. As pioneer river towns and beyond grew in the first half of the 19th century, so did the demand for lumber and building materials. The lush forests of the upper Mississippi Valley satisfied this seemingly endless need for decades. (Courtesy of Muscatine Art Center.)

LOG RAFT, C. 1890. Once harvested, logs often traveled long distances to mill towns along the Mississippi River. Initially lumber was floated down the water on large rafts. In smaller tributaries, men walked along the shore and pulled the rafts with hand lines. Sails and teams of men with large oars were also used to deliver the timber to its final destination. (Courtesy of Muscatine Art Center.)

B. Hershey Log Raft and Lotus Cargo of Shells, 1880s. Steamboats began pushing log rafts down the Mississippi River in the 1850s. Local lumber barons built their own steamboats to improve timber delivery. The Hershey Lumber Company owned the B. *Hershey*, named after founder Benjamin Hershey. In 1879, the B. *Hershey* propelled one of the largest log rafts to date down the Mississippi River. The raft measured 310 feet by 535 feet. (Courtesy of Musser Public Library.)

Steamer Urania Docked on Muscatine Riverfront after Fire, 1901. Steamboats quickly became a popular mode of transportation in the 1800s. However, early steamboats were not regulated, and boiler explosions were a constant worry. In 1837, the steamer *Dubuque* exploded on the Mississippi River south of Muscatine, killing 22 people. The victims were originally buried at Seventh and Orange Streets, but they were reburied in Greenwood Cemetery to make way for a new school. (Courtesy of Muscatine Art Center.)

MUSCATINE HIGH BRIDGE, 1909. The Muscatine Bridge Company organized in 1888 with the goal of spanning the Mississippi River between Muscatine and Rock Island County, Illinois. Its capital stock was $50,000; Peter Miller Musser served as president. The Youngstown Bridge Company and Milwaukee Bridge and Iron Company began construction on July 15, 1889. (Courtesy of Musser Public Library.)

VIEW OF MUSCATINE FROM THE TOP OF THE HIGH BRIDGE, c. 1915. Early concepts envisioned a two-level structure to accommodate both horse and railroad traffic. The plans were abandoned and the single-level High Bridge opened to traffic on May 7, 1891. The structure measured just over 3,101 feet from landing to landing. Its longest span was 442 feet. (Courtesy of Musser Public Library.)

HIGH BRIDGE COLLAPSE, 1899. One span of the High Bridge collapsed on February 4, 1899. The accident claimed the lives of two horses that were hauling cargo across the bridge, but the drivers escaped serious injury. The same span collapsed again in June 1956. The old High Bridge was dynamited on April 5, 1973. A single pylon in Riverside Park is all that remains of the High Bridge. (Courtesy of Muscatine Art Center.)

WALNUT STREET TOLL BOOTH, 1910. A tollbooth opened on the Walnut Street end of the High Bridge in 1891. In this photograph, Tony Christian and Andrew Fryberger stand near the doorway of the tollbooth. The McKibben House, which now serves as offices of the Greater Muscatine Chamber of Commerce and Industry, can be seen in the background. (Courtesy of Muscatine Art Center.)

"THE SWEET HOUSE," C. 1910. The Fryberger family also worked the tollbooth on the Illinois side of the High Bridge. Dubbed the "Sweet House," bridge passengers could purchase a wide range of items for their journey, including "ice cold drinks and lemonade," firecrackers, stamps, "marsh-mallows," and tobacco products. (Courtesy of Muscatine Art Center.)

ANDREW FRYBERGER WITH "JO.JO." THE MONKEY, 1933. Andrew Fryberger collected High Bridge tolls for nearly 45 years. For many years, a monkey named Joe (also known as Jo.Jo.) was known to chat with and entertain bridge crossers. (Courtesy of Muscatine Art Center.)

THE *HELEN BLAIR* STEAMS PAST MUSCATINE, C. 1905. Steamboat packet lines, including White Collar, Diamond Jo, Northern, and Carnival City, once linked Muscatine to communities along the Mississippi River. The white-banded smokestacks of the *Helen Blair*, seen here in the foreground, signal the paddle wheel operated as part of the White Collar Packet Line. The Northern Packet Line's steamers included the *Muscatine*. (Courtesy of Muscatine Art Center.)

MISSISSIPPI RIVER FLOOD, 1903. Mother Nature ultimately controls the Mississippi River. Numerous flood events have been recorded in Muscatine's history. In 1903, residents watched helplessly as the water raged across the riverfront near the Cedar Street intersection. The modern-day Mississippi River flood stage in Muscatine is 16 feet. The highest recorded local crest was 25.61 feet on July 9, 1993. (Courtesy of Musser Public Library.)

ICE-CUTTING MACHINE, 1906. Before refrigeration was common, ice was harvested for year-round use when the Mississippi River and other area waterways froze over in the winter. Ice blocks were cut by hand, an ice saw, or a power-driven cutter. Once harvested, the blocks were sent to an icehouse for storage and packed with sawdust to keep it from melting well into the summer months. (Courtesy of Muscatine Art Center.)

PURITAN ICE COMPANY OF MUSCATINE COUPON BOOK, c. 1919. The ice "cakes" were first delivered by horse-drawn carts and carried with large ice tongs. Customers could order ice by displaying their "ice card" in the front window. Coupon books, such as the one pictured here, were also used. (Courtesy of Muscatine Art Center.)

LOCK AND DAM NO. 16 CONSTRUCTION, 1935. The U.S. Army Corps of Engineers began the mammoth task of taming the Mississippi for modern river traffic in the 1930s. Lock and Dam No. 16, on the Illinois side of the river east of Muscatine, opened in July 1937. It was one of 29 built along the Upper Mississippi River Valley, stretching from St. Anthony Falls, Minnesota, to Granite City, Illinois. (Courtesy of Musser Public Library.)

Three

Lumber, Buttons, and Melons

South Muscatine Lumber Company, 1904. The prospect of fortune drew pioneers westward in the early 1800s, and enterprising businessmen in the Upper Mississippi River Valley built sawmills to meet the lumber demand of new settlers. Lumber transformed Muscatine's economy in the latter half of the 19th century. River mussels and agricultural products further helped to cement Muscatine's place in history. (Courtesy of Musser Public Library.)

SOUTH MUSCATINE LUMBER DISTRICT, 1890S. Muscatine was a major Midwest lumber hub by the mid-1860s. In 1865, more than 13 million feet of lumber, six million shingles, and four million laths were shipped by rail or river. History references dozens of local lumber mills and corporations, but the operations owned by the Hershey, Musser, Roach, and Huttig families stood out above the rest. (Courtesy of Muscatine Art Center.)

HERSHEY MILL, C. 1860. Pennsylvania farmer and tobacco merchant Benjamin Hershey first visited Muscatine to find land to establish a dairy farm. By the mid-1850s, Hershey owned a farm just west of Muscatine and rented a small riverfront sawmill, originally built by his cousin. Hershey parlayed these businesses into a corporation worth millions of dollars. (Courtesy of Muscatine Art Center.)

HERSHEY'S UPPER MILL, 1901. Benjamin Hershey's first mill was primitive but efficient. He used the profits to construct a larger mill in the mid-1850s along the Muscatine Slough near the present-day intersection of Hershey and Grandview Avenues. By the 1860s, this new mill was capable of producing 225,000 board feet of lumber in 24 hours. (Courtesy of Muscatine Art Center.)

SOUTH MUSCATINE MAP, 1856. Benjamin Hershey's new "upper" mill was located in the area then known as South Muscatine. The location was prone to flooding, and the dusty spoils of Hershey's operation and other lumber mills provided the base on which the "Sloughtown" neighborhood was founded. (Courtesy of Muscatine Art Center.)

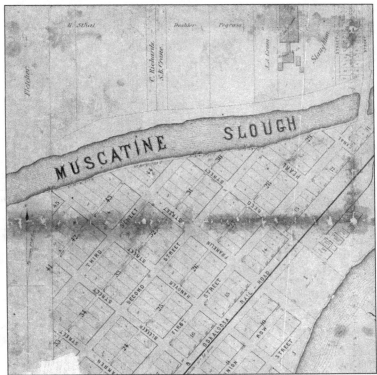

PRICE LIST.

HERSHEY

LUMBER COMPANY,

MANUFACTURERS AND
WHOLESALE DEALERS

—IN—

LUMBER, LATH,

SHINGLES

AND PICKETS.

ESTABLISHED 1853.
INCORPORATED 1875.
CHARTER EXTENDED 1895.

HERSHEY LUMBER CATALOG COVER, C. 1896. In 1875, Benjamin Hershey partnered with local entrepreneur and furniture maker Simon G. Stein to form the Hershey Lumber Company. By 1889, the corporation owned two local mills and another in Stillwater, Minnesota. Annual profits approached the $1 million mark. Benjamin Hershey died in 1893, and the upper mill closed in 1902. (Courtesy of Muscatine Art Center.)

SOUTH MUSCATINE LUMBER COMPANY, 1904. John Kaiser and L. C. Lenck partnered to open the South Muscatine Lumber Company on the former site of Benjamin Hershey's "lower" mill on Oregon Street. In 1900, South Muscatine Lumber Company processed 35 million feet of lumber, employed over 350 workers, and recorded $750,000 in annual sales. (Courtesy of Musser Public Library.)

PETER MUSSER, 1911.
Brothers Peter and Richard
Musser moved to Iowa
in the early 1850s and,
together with other family
members, helped form
one of Muscatine's largest
lumber empires. Both men
briefly settled in Iowa City
and there partnered with
Muscatine businessman
Edward Hoch to form the
lumber company Hoch
and Musser. The company
operated a mill in Muscatine
and a lumberyard in
Iowa City. (Courtesy of
Muscatine Art Center.)

PETER MILLER MUSSER, C. 1905.
Richard Musser eventually moved
to Muscatine and started Richard
Musser and Company when Edward
Hoch retired in 1857. Musser's nephew
Peter Miller Musser bought into the
company and assumed management
of the Iowa City operation. Peter
Miller Musser later sold his interest
in the Iowa City lumberyard and
joined his uncles in organizing the
Musser and Company lumber firm.
(Courtesy of Musser Public Library.)

BOAT MUSSER, 1897. The Musser family success, in part, can be attributed to its ability to secure a steady supply of lumber. As Iowa's timberlands depleted, the Mussers purchased logging interests in the Pacific Northwest. The businessmen also joined forces with Rock Island County, Illinois, entrepreneur Frederick Weyerhaeuser and others in 1872 to operate the Mississippi River Logging Company. Weyerhaeuser later founded the paper company that still bears his name. (Courtesy of Muscatine Art Center.)

ROACH AND MUSSER SASH AND DOOR FRAME, VENEER AND DOOR B WORKERS, 1938. Work in the lumber mills was grueling. An 1880 industrial census concluded the average workday lasted 11 hours. Laborers were paid an average of $1.50 per day; skilled laborers could make an average of $2 more daily. Musser and Company was reincorporated as the Musser Lumber Company in 1881. (Courtesy of Muscatine Art Center.)

32

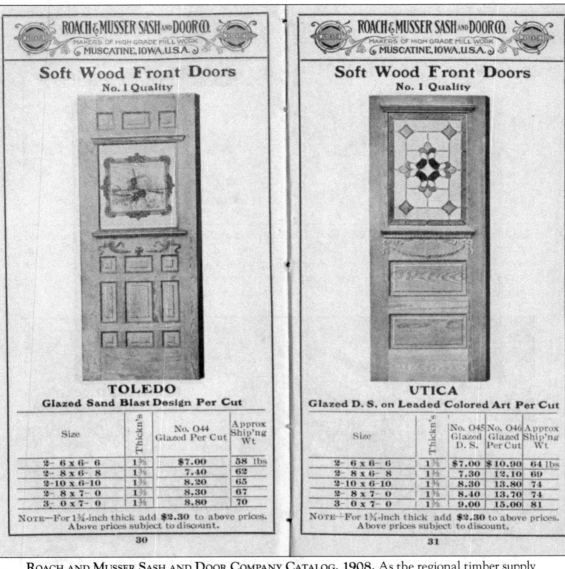

Soft Wood Front Doors
No. 1 Quality

TOLEDO
Glazed Sand Blast Design Per Cut

Size	Thickn's	No. O44 Glazed Per Cut	Approx Ship'ng Wt
2- 6 x 6- 6	1⅜	$7.00	58 lbs
2- 8 x 6- 8	1⅜	7.40	62
2-10 x 6-10	1⅜	8.20	65
2- 8 x 7- 0	1⅜	8.30	67
3- 0 x 7- 0	1⅜	8.80	70

NOTE—For 1¾-inch thick add **$2.30** to above prices.
Above prices subject to discount.

30

Soft Wood Front Doors
No. 1 Quality

UTICA
Glazed D. S. on Leaded Colored Art Per Cut

Size	Thickn's	No. O45 Glazed D. S.	No. O46 Glazed Per Cut	Approx Ship'ng Wt
2- 6 x 6- 6	1⅜	$7.00	$10.90	64 lbs
2- 8 x 6- 8	1⅜	7.30	12.10	69
2-10 x 6-10	1⅜	8.30	13.80	74
2- 8 x 7- 0	1⅜	8.40	13.70	74
3- 0 x 7- 0	1⅜	9.00	15.00	81

NOTE—For 1¾-inch thick add **$2.30** to above prices.
Above prices subject to discount.

31

ROACH AND MUSSER SASH AND DOOR COMPANY CATALOG, 1908. As the regional timber supply decreased, Muscatine's lumber companies increasingly shifted manufacturing to include doors, sashes, blinds, moldings, stairs, mantles, and other home-building materials. The switch proved successful, and before the beginning of the 20th century Muscatine's lumber giants had expanded product lines and out-of-state operations. (Courtesy of Muscatine Art Center.)

ROACH AND MUSSER SASH AND DOOR COMPANY LETTERHEAD, 1882. In 1889, the Mussers purchased a floundering lumberyard and organized the Muscatine Sash and Door Company with William Roach. The business name was later changed to Roach and Musser Sash and Door Company. The Musser family's local enterprise grew so expansive, the area surrounding the South Muscatine facilities earned the moniker "Musserville." (Courtesy of Muscatine Art Center.)

WILLIAM ROACH FAMILY, C. 1900. William Roach cut his teeth in the lumber business working for the Huttig family, one of the four dominant lumber families of Muscatine. He started his career at age 18 as a bookkeeper for his father's shoe store. Roach later moved to Kansas City to manage the Huttig family's operation there. In this photograph, William Roach (far right) poses with his family. (Courtesy of Musser Public Library.)

ROACH AND MUSSER SASH AND DOOR COMPANY, C. 1900. Roach and Musser, "The Makers of Everything in Millwork," manufactured from its location on Grandview Avenue. At its peak, the manufacturing facility covered more than a dozen acres and employed hundreds. Roach and Musser also owned and operated a branch location in Kansas City, Missouri, named Roach and Musser and Riner Manufacturing Company. Multiple fires devastated large sections of the Muscatine plant site after the beginning of the 20th century. One 1912 blaze reportedly burned for two days and took six million gallons of water to extinguish. The company was rebuilt and was sold to a New York firm in 1957. It was then purchased by a Muscatine company in 1963 and closed for good a few years later. (Courtesy of Muscatine Art Center.)

WILLIAM HUTTIG, 1860s. German immigrants William and Charles Frederick Huttig arrived in Muscatine to pursue careers as an architect and music teacher, respectively. Economic necessity forced both to become skilled stonemasons. During the Civil War, the brothers opened a grocery and feed store on Second Street near Chestnut Street. (Courtesy of Musser Public Library.)

BIRD'S-EYE VIEW OF HUTTIG MANUFACTURING COMPANY, C. 1890. William and Charles Frederick Huttig's ascension into the ranks as one of Muscatine's most successful lumber families began in 1868 with the purchase of a local mill. The brothers soon added a second operation in Kellogg, west of Grinnell, Iowa. (Courtesy of Musser Public Library.)

HUTTIG MANUFACTURING PLANT, 1928. The central Iowa lumberyard was eventually sold and Huttig Brothers Manufacturing Company formed in the 1870s. The name was changed to Huttig Manufacturing Company in 1881. The company's operations, based at 701 East Second Street, soon occupied more than six square blocks as demand for its doors and window frames increased. (Courtesy of Muscatine Art Center.)

HUTTIG MANUFACTURING POCKET CATALOG, c. 1908. Harry Huttig, the son of William, took charge of the family operation when his father was out of town. During one leadership stint, Harry developed a front door design that was different from those universally advertised. The design proved so popular that Huttig recruited more than 100 local carpenters to carve the intricate blocks of wood for the door panels. (Courtesy of Muscatine Art Center.)

HUTTIG MANUFACTURING PLANT, C. 1916. Success propelled the Huttig family to open the Western Sash and Door Company in Kansas City, Missouri, in 1883. A second location, the Huttig Sash and Door Company, was added in St. Louis, Missouri, in 1885. It continues to operate today under the name Huttig Building Products, Inc. Huttig Manufacturing remained one of Muscatine's largest companies well into the second half of the 20th century. HON Industries purchased its facilities in the 1970s. (Courtesy of Muscatine Art Center.)

SHELL BARGE *BUTTERFLY* ON THE MISSISSIPPI RIVER, C. 1910. Although Huttig Manufacturing and Roach and Musser continued to produce building products well into the 20th century, the original sawmills that made Muscatine a regional lumber hub had all but shuttered by 1905. However, the tough shell of river mussels transformed the community into the world's largest button manufacturer. (Courtesy of Muscatine Art Center.)

FREDERICK BOEPPLE CUTTING SHELLS, C. 1891. German immigrant John Frederick Boepple dreamed of pearly shells when he arrived in the United States. He discovered his dream in the thick mussels found in the Mississippi River near Muscatine. In 1891, Boepple opened a factory and launched the local pearl button industry. Residents questioned the factory's viability, but Muscatine would soon become the Pearl Button Capital of the World. (Courtesy of Muscatine Art Center.)

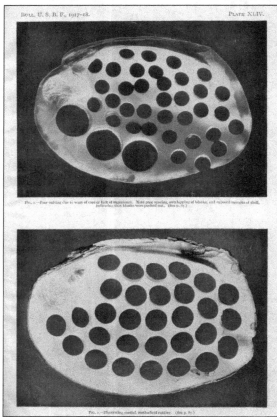

CLAMMER WITH SCISSOR FORKS, C. 1920. The journey of a pearl button began under water. Mussels were harvested from the Mississippi and other regional rivers. Some clammers would drag the riverbeds using hooks attached to ropes and chains secured to metal bars. Others used scissor forks sometimes known as clam rakes. This image was the inspiration for the *Mississippi Harvest* sculpture installed in Riverside Park in 2006. (Courtesy of Muscatine Art Center.)

CUT SHELLS, C. 1919. The mussels were cleaned and boiled, and the shells were then ready to be cut into blanks. John Boepple initially used a foot-powered lathe to cut the shells and then carve and drill buttons. The carving and drilling process was later automated. (Courtesy of Muscatine History and Industry Center.)

BARRY MANUFACTURING, C. 1915. The growth of Muscatine's button industry was fueled, in part, by the inventions of the Barry family. A visit to Henry Umlandt's button operation inspired brothers John and Nicholas Barry to engineer an automatic cutting machine in 1900. This single machine soon spurred a line of manufacturing devices that transformed and modernized the button industry. (Courtesy of Musser Public Library.)

DOUBLE AUTOMATIC MACHINE, C. 1920. Grinding machines removed the outer shell, or bark, of the mussel from the blank. Blanks were then fed into machines that drilled holes and cut the button pattern. By 1904, the process became more uniform and economical with the introduction of Barry Manufacturing's Double Automatic machine. During peak years, Muscatine companies produced 1.5 billion buttons a year. (Courtesy of Muscatine History and Industry Center.)

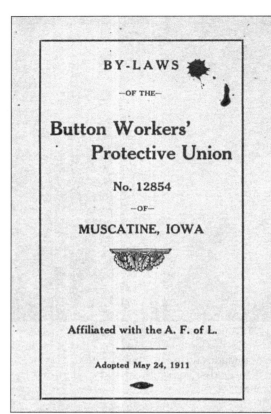

BUTTON UNION BYLAWS, 1911. The button industry employed nearly half of the local workforce in its heyday. Low wages, unsafe conditions, and high tool costs prompted strikes. The first local button union organized in 1899, but the movement did not take hold until an affiliation with the American Federation of Labor (AFL) was established in 1910. (Courtesy of Muscatine Art Center.)

ARMED MILITIA IN DOWNTOWN MUSCATINE, 1911. Citing overproduction and low demand, 43 local button operations shut down in February 1911. The union called the action a lockout and within days started picket lines. Tension grew between members of the Button Workers' Protective Union and non-union workers. In April, Muscatine was placed under martial law for four days. (Courtesy of Musser Public Library.)

WEED PARK BUTTON UNION MEETING, 1911. Iowa governor Beryl Franklin Carroll helped negotiate a settlement in May 1911, and union members returned to work. The truce did not last long. The union declared a general strike in September. The strike did not effectively end until the union issued a statement on May 22, 1912. (Courtesy of Musser Public Library.)

BUTTON CARD, 1920s. Local button manufacturing peaked in the mid-1910s. The boom turned to bust over the next decades as overharvesting depleted mussel supplies and the popularity of less expensive plastic buttons increased. Local pearl button production ended in the 1960s. Only three of the scores of businesses that once supported Muscatine's button dynasty remain: McKee Button Company, J and K Button Company, and Weber and Sons Button Company. (Courtesy of Muscatine Art Center.)

EMERSON HOOPES'S PUMPKIN FIELD, 1912. Lumber and pearl buttons dominated industry during Muscatine's first 100 years, but produce harvested by farmers on the Muscatine Island also gained a national reputation. The island was once completely separated from the mainland by the Mississippi Slough. (Courtesy of Musser Public Library.)

IOWA, 1845. The first settlement on the 27,000-acre Muscatine Island was recorded in 1836. A rope-pulled ferry across the slough connected the Island to Bloomington (Muscatine) in the late 1830s. A dam constructed in 1845 served as the first connecting road to the mainland. (Courtesy of Muscatine Art Center.)

Muscatine Canning Label. The Muscatine Island's sandy soil made the land ideal for melon, fruit, and vegetable growing. In the mid-1870s, William Henry Hoopes established his Island Garden farm. Hoopes started wholesale gardening, believing the Island's bounty could be shipped and sold beyond the immediate Muscatine area. (Courtesy of Muscatine Art Center.)

Fruitland Watermelon "Feed," 1895. The 1880 arrival of a Rock Island Railroad depot in the town of Fruitland provided a new avenue to ship fresh produce. By the end of the 1880 growing season, 30 rail cars had hauled melons and other produce from the island. The Muscatine Island–grown watermelon and cantaloupe-variety muskmelons soon gained national fame for their unique sweet taste. (Courtesy of Muscatine Art Center.)

MELON CRATES AT RAIL DEPOT, 1920. There were 2,500 acres of Muscatine County land dedicated to watermelon and cantaloupe production by 1921. In addition to melons, Island produce included sweet potatoes, tomatoes, and cabbage. Today a handful of farms continue the island's agricultural tradition, and Muscatine melons remain a desired summer treat. (Courtesy of Musser Public Library.)

Four

CITY TRANSFORMATION

MUSCATINE, 1875. Immediately after Bloomington (Muscatine) was incorporated in 1839, local leaders swiftly undertook projects to transform the pioneer town into a full-fledged river city. Bloomington served as the seat for the Muscatine County government. Within months, a courthouse and jail were operational. This lithograph prominently features the *Muscatine* steamer of the Northern Packet Line and the ferry *Ida May*. (Courtesy of Muscatine Art Center.)

Jail.
MUSCATINE IA.

Court House, Muscatine. Ia.

MUSCATINE COUNTY JAIL, C. 1909. The first jail was built near the Fourth and Walnut Streets intersection in 1839. It is believed to be the first county building constructed within Muscatine city limits. It was replaced with a multistory brick building on Fourth Street in 1857. In 1907, a limestone jail was erected at the corner of Fourth and Walnut. This jail cost $21,000 and included sheriff's housing. This facility housed prisoners until the current jail opened in 1996. (Courtesy of Muscatine Art Center.)

COURTHOUSE, C. 1866. Ground for the first courthouse was purchased in a public land sale in 1839; Muscatine County paid the federal government $1.25 per acre. The courthouse opened the following year but burned to the ground in 1864. The courthouse was reconstructed with a 20-foot-by-70-foot addition for nearly $30,000 in 1866.

COURTHOUSE CONSTRUCTION, C. **1909.** Construction on the current courthouse began in 1907. The county sold $150,000 in bonds to finance the new courthouse, as well as a new jail facility at the corner of Fourth and Walnut Streets. The bonds were sold to European investors, as financial conditions made the bonds difficult to sell domestically. The present building sits in the center of the courthouse square (bound by Walnut, Fourth, and Third Streets and Mulberry Avenue), placing it just feet from the 1866 courthouse location. Six pillars and a porch had to be removed from the 1866 building in order to complete the new courthouse. The 1866 courthouse was completely demolished when the current building was completed. The first court session in the present courthouse was held on June 9, 1909. (Courtesy of Musser Public Library.)

MUSCATINE CITY HALL, 1877. In 1856, the city council chambers were located over Green and Stone's Bank on Second Street. Twenty years later, the city purchased the old Methodist Church at the corner of Third and Sycamore Streets for $2,500 and converted the building into city hall. (Courtesy of Musser Public Library.)

MUSCATINE CITY HALL, C. 1915. In 1913, Muscatine's electorate supported a bond issue for a new city hall. The location was subject of great debate, but local leaders settled on a site directly across the street from the old building. The three-story limestone city hall was dedicated in 1915 and continues to serve as the primary location for city business. (Courtesy of Muscatine Art Center.)

MUSSER PUBLIC LIBRARY, 1912. Peter Miller Musser donated the land and $50,000 necessary to construct the first library building. Citizens overwhelmingly approved a $1 million tax levy to support and maintain the institution. (Courtesy of Musser Public Library.)

MUSSER PUBLIC LIBRARY INTERIOR, C. 1902. The red sandstone building, located at Third Street and Iowa Avenue, officially opened in February 1902. The library featured reading rooms and a separate children's section. *Elizabeth and Her German Garden* was the first book borrowed. A rear addition was added in 1965, but the entire structure was razed in 1971 to make way for a modern library. (Courtesy of Musser Public Library.)

POST OFFICE, C. 1915. Edward E. Fay served as Bloomington's (Muscatine's) first postmaster. He was appointed to the position in 1837. Early postmasters were political appointees and changed often. The office name change to Muscatine coincided with the town's name change in 1849. Up until the post office building was constructed, mail was housed in a number of downtown locations. (Courtesy of Muscatine Art Center.)

MAIL DELIVERY, 1905. City delivery service began in 1887 with four carriers under the leadership of postmaster George W. Van Horn. The same year the post office moved to the Fitzgerald Building on the 100 block of Iowa Avenue. A portion of Missipi Brewing Company now operates out of the ground floor of the Fitzgerald Building. (Courtesy of Musser Public Library.)

Muscatine Post Office Interior, 1909. Postmaster Robert McNutt oversaw the construction of a new post office at the corner of Iowa Avenue and Fourth Street in 1908. The new facility boasted indoor plumbing and gas lighting. A 1930s renovation doubled the building's size. It served as the main post office until 1998 when a modern post office opened at the corner of Cedar and Houser Streets. (Courtesy of Musser Public Library.)

MUSCATINE WATER WORKS, C. 1877. Muscatine Water Works opened in 1876 as the first water company to serve the city. The privately held business secured a 25-year franchise to furnish water to the city. It utilized a pump house on Chestnut Street to draw water directly from the Mississippi River. Eleven miles of water mains and more than 100 fire hydrants were installed by 1900. (Courtesy of Muscatine Art Center.)

MAPLE GROVE PUMPING STATION, 1906. Seeking a safer water supply, the Muscatine City Council, with the backing of a community referendum, purchased Muscatine Water Works in 1900 for $100,000. The new municipal utility purchased land from the Hoopes family on the Muscatine Island. Six years later, a new pumping station was completed on Maple Grove Road. (Courtesy of Musser Public Library.)

WATER METER TESTING ROOM, 1920s.
Water was drawn from the island's clean
aquifer via multiple wells instead of
directly from the Mississippi River. Early
water rates were $6 a year for homes with
four rooms. By 1916, water meters had
been installed throughout the city and
a 250,000-gallon water tower was in use
near Kindler Avenue and Cook Street.
(Courtesy of Muscatine Power and Water.)

PAPOOSE CREEK EXTENSION, 1905. Papoose Creek, one of two small streams that flow through
Muscatine, once divided portions of the city. Bridges aided downtown transportation until a
large sewer placed underneath Sycamore Street in 1895 encased part of Papoose Creek. The
sewer was later extended, effectively placing the stream underground. (Courtesy of Musser
Public Library.)

CITIZEN'S RAILWAY AND LIGHT POWER HOUSE, NEAR FRONT (MISSISSIPPI DRIVE) AND OAK STREETS, 1908. Citizens Electric Light and Power Company formed in 1890. Within a year, the first generation plant was built at the corner of Front (Mississippi Drive) and Pine Streets, and the electricity produced could power 1,600 incandescent lights. The utility vacated this plant in 1892 after a fire at the nearby Stein Lumber Company. The plant later moved to near Front and Oak Streets, and the company went through a series of name changes until it ceased operations in the 1920s. During its heyday, Citizens Electric Light and Power Company also offered gas service, reportedly selling gas stoves at cost and providing free connection service. The original plant at Front and Pine subsequently housed a series of button companies, a produce operation, and a vermin trap factory. It is now home to J and K Button Company. (Courtesy of Musser Public Library.)

THE 300 BLOCK OF SECOND STREET AT NIGHT, 1928. Although Citizens Electric Light and Power Company had local management, it was dependent on the generators owned by Quad Cities investors. After a series of ownership changes, Citizens Electric emerged as the Muscatine Lighting Company. Plans for a competitor, in the form of a municipal electric utility, came together after voters approved a $350,000 referendum in 1922. (Courtesy of Muscatine Art Center.)

MUNICIPAL LIGHT PLANT CONSTRUCTION, 1923. The board of trustees for Muscatine's municipal electric utility was formed in 1922. Money generated from the newly approved bond sale was used to build a power plant adjacent to the municipal water facility on Maple Grove Road. The plant went online in 1924, and former Muscatine mayor Joseph Miller was issued the municipal utility's first electric meter. (Courtesy of Musser Public Library.)

WEST HILL RESERVOIR, C. 1916. State legislation made it possible for the two municipal utilities to merge into Muscatine Power and Light in 1929. The name was changed to Muscatine Power and Water in 1967. The public utility continues to supply the city's electric and water needs, as well as Internet and cable television service. (Courtesy of Muscatine Power and Water.)

CHAMPION HOSE, HOOK, AND LADDER COMPANY ARTICLES OF INCORPORATION, 1898. Private and volunteer fire companies fought blazes in Muscatine until 1875. Gustav Schmidt organized the first fire company in January 1875. Forty men volunteered for the "German Fire Company." A few months later, the unit was known as the Champion Chemical Fire Company. The name was later changed to Champion Hose, Hook, and Ladder Company No. 1. (Courtesy of Muscatine Art Center.)

FIRST CONGREGATIONAL CHURCH FIRE, 1907. The first organized department initially fought blazes with chemical fire extinguishers, although the results were often less than desirable. As Muscatine Water Works introduced a city system, firefighters abandoned the chemical fire extinguishers in 1876 and switched to using hand-drawn hose carts and a hook-and-ladder wagon. (Courtesy of Muscatine Art Center.)

MUSCATINE FIRE DEPARTMENT ON FRONT STREET (MISSISSIPPI DRIVE), 1878. Three more fire units were created over the next two years. The Relief Hook and Ladder Company formed in April 1877. This unit worked alongside the Champion Hose Company located at 308 Sycamore Street. (Courtesy of Muscatine Art Center.)

RESCUE HOSE COMPANY NO. 2, C. 1900. Rescue Hose Company No. 2 formed in April 1876 and moved to 421 Mulberry Avenue in 1877 (the current Veterans of Foreign Wars building). Excelsior Hose Company No. 3 formed in June 1876 and provided initial service from a location on Broadway Street. The company later moved to Third Street before relocating to 321 Cherry Street in 1913. The Relief Hose Company No. 4, initially based at 700 Bismarck Street (now Liberty Street), organized in March 1888. The company later moved to the 200 block of Bleeker Street. (Courtesy of Muscatine Art Center.)

HUTTIG FIRE BRIGADE, 1903. Several Muscatine lumberyards maintained private fire brigades. The Hershey Hose Company organized in 1880. Huttig Manufacturing and Kaiser Lumber Company also had private fire brigades. Roach and Musser Company formed its hose company in 1886. (Courtesy of Muscatine Art Center.)

PETER MILLER MUSSER WITH MUSCATINE FIRE TRUCK, 1913. Lumber baron Peter Miller Musser gifted Muscatine's first motorized fire truck in 1913. The American LaFrance truck was reportedly made with solid tires that would not deflate while racing over the city's rough roads. Firefighters proudly demonstrated the new rig by racing to League Field and unfurling hoses. Peter Miller Musser is sitting next to the driver in this photograph. (Courtesy of Muscatine Art Center.)

Muscatine Fire Department at City Hall, c. 1934. The city of Muscatine hired its first two paid firefighters in 1913. Two years later, the city council passed an ordinance that effectively organized a paid department of 12 men plus a fire chief. Volunteer brigades disbanded early the next year. Over the next three decades, the fire department manned station houses on Sycamore

Street, Cherry Street, and Hershey Avenue. The Cherry Street and Hershey Avenue stations were closed by the late 1940s. The Oregon Street substation was added in 1949. The Public Safety Building on Fifth Street was built in 1976 and today serves as the main firehouse and police station. (Courtesy of Muscatine Art Center.)

POLICE DEPARTMENT IN FRONT OF MUSCATINE CITY HALL, 1934. Bloomington's (Muscatine's) first police marshal was appointed in 1839. Muscatine patrol officer Thomas D. Moore became the state of Iowa's first recorded police officer killed in the line of duty. On July 12, 1869, Moore died when he was struck by lightning while walking his assigned beat near East Ninth and Oak Streets, also known as Ogilvie's Hill. Police officer Theodore Gerischer was killed during the 1911 button industry's labor strife. In November, Gerischer was questioning a group of young men suspected of causing a disturbance near West Third and Spruce Streets. As one ran from the scene, Gerischer fired a warning shot. The man returned fire and Gerischer died of a head

wound the next day. Two additional local officers have died protecting the city. Officer Jake Neibert was shot and killed near the Hershey Train Platform in 1896. Assistant chief Menzo Grady died in 1947 responding to a soapbox derby accident. The department welcomed its first permanent headquarters when the new city hall was finished in 1915. Officers operated from the ground level, which today houses the city's parks and recreation department. The police department has been located in the Public Safety Building at Cedar and Fifth Streets since the 1970s. (Courtesy of Muscatine Police Department.)

ROCK ISLAND AND PACIFIC TRAIN ENGINE IN MUSCATINE, C. 1900. The first train to operate in Iowa powered its way to Muscatine on November 10, 1855. A three-day celebration greeted the *Excursion*, which arrived from Davenport on tracks owned by the Mississippi and Missouri Railroad Company (M&M). The Chicago, Rock Island, and Pacific Railroad absorbed M&M in 1866. By 1889, multiple companies provided passenger and freight service to Muscatine. (Courtesy of Musser Public Library.)

MUSCATINE NORTH AND SOUTH RAILROAD WRECK NEAR GRANDVIEW, 1909. The Muscatine North and South Railroad Company (MN&S) organized in 1897. This short-line operation initially stretched 28 miles from Muscatine south to near present-day Oakville, Iowa. Track was later extended to Burlington, but the railway went bankrupt. After a few ownership changes, the remnants of the MN&S were sold to the Rock Island Line. (Courtesy of Musser Public Library.)

OGILVIE HOUSE, C. 1866. The earliest passenger depot operated from the Ogilvie House, later known as the Commercial House, on Front Street (Mississippi Drive). A train passenger station originally built in Durant, Iowa, was moved in 1866 to the corner of Linn and Front Streets. Fire gutted the wood structure in 1881, but it was repaired and continued to serve passengers until after the beginning of the 20th century. (Courtesy of Muscatine Art Center.)

UNION STATION, C. 1910. The first brick depot was erected near the Front Street (Mississippi Drive) train tracks near Iowa Avenue in 1905. Known as Union Station, the depot was razed in 1962. Six years later, the Rock Island Line discontinued local passenger service. (Courtesy of Muscatine Art Center.)

HORSE-DRAWN STREETCAR AT THIRD STREET AND MULBERRY AVENUE, 1889. Muscatine's foray into public transit began in the 1880s. The newly formed Muscatine City Railway Company introduced the first streetcar in 1883. The early cars were powered by horse and mule. By 1890, more than 2 miles of track serviced heavily populated neighborhoods, the downtown district, and other popular destinations. (Courtesy of Musser Public Library.)

STREET CAR AT ELECTRIC PARK, C. 1915. The first electric streetcar powered its way along Mulberry Avenue in May 1893. Operated by the Citizen's Electric Railway and Light Company, the electric trolleys ran on 15-horsepower engines. A coal plant at the corner of Oak and Front (Mississippi Drive) Streets supplied the necessary electricity. Cars were marked "Muscatine Electric Railway," and the initial fare was 5¢. (Courtesy of the Musser Public Library.)

East Second and Cedar Streets Intersection, c. 1906. The early streetcar passenger depot was located at 220 Iowa Avenue. Initially streetcars were housed and serviced at the corner of Third Street and Mulberry Avenue until a massive fire tore through the building in 1903, destroying 25 cars. The maintenance barn then moved to a new building at the corner of Third and Oak Streets. (Courtesy of Muscatine Art Center.)

Interurban Time Table, 1917. Multiple electric railway routes snaked through Muscatine on nearly 11 miles of track by 1914. Traveling via streetcar became possible between Davenport and Muscatine in 1912. Four years later, the expanded Clinton, Davenport, and Muscatine Railway line (CD&M) formed. Larger electric cars of this interurban service made dozens of stops between the three cities on tracks separate from those used by steam railroad companies. (Courtesy of Muscatine Art Center.)

GEOGRAPHICAL LIST OF STATIONS
C. D. & M. RAILWAY

DAVENPORT	DAVENPORT
BETTENDORF	Blackhawk
Zimmerman	Fairmont
Davis Gardens	Peterson
Nuttings	Cawiezel
Iowana	Schupp
Fennos	Steenbolt
Schutter	Hetzel
PLEAS. VALLEY	Coates
Mason	Gubbert
McArthurs	Barnes
Alta Ripa	Bruce
Snell	BLUE GRASS
Tile Works	Schroeder
Riverview	Nicholson
Smiths	Drum
Sutter	Aibee
Sharon	Baker
LE CLAIRE	PLEASANT PRAIRIE
Walnut Street	Stocker
L. & J. PARK	Paul
Hopsons	Kelley
Cottage Grove	Melpine
Budd Creek	Pine Creek
PRINCETON	RAINBOW
Toby	Van Camp
School House Road	SWEETLAND
W. Public Highway	Hatfield
Wapsie	Sherfey
Folletts	Richman
SHAFFTON	City Limits
Oakes Park	MUSCATINE
Rock Creek	
CAMANCHE	
Fenlons	
Power House	
Car Barn	
CLINTON	

INTERURBAN TIME TABLE

EFFECTIVE MARCH 1ST, 1917

Clinton, Davenport and Muscatine Ry.

1851 – 1879

DISTRICT NO. 2 SCHOOL, 1850s. John A. Parvin rented a cabin in Muscatine and opened the first school in the county in 1839. By 1848, the city was divided into two school districts on either side of Sycamore Street. District No. 2 opened its first school in 1851 on Third Street between Spruce and Locust Streets. Classes at the District No. 1 School, at the corner of Seventh and Orange Streets, began in 1853. One year later, Finley Miller Witter started formally organizing local schools. Witter later served in a variety of capacities, including principal and superintendent, until he retired in 1901. (Courtesy of Musser Public Library.)

MUSCATINE HIGH SCHOOL, C. 1900. Construction on the first Muscatine High School commenced in 1873 at the corner of Sycamore and Orange Streets, the site of the former District No. 1 School. Fire destroyed the multistory brick building, designed by local resident Josiah P. Walton, in February 1896. A more modern building was erected at the corner of Iowa Avenue and Sixth Street later the same year. The first classes in the $30,000 high school were held in January 1897. This high school became known as Central Junior High School in 1939. The City of Muscatine purchased the old Central Junior High School in 1976, and the building was razed in October 1978 to make way for what is now the Tower Apartments. The school's large bell, the only item spared from the wrecking ball, now greets visitors as they drive into the current high school complex from Cedar Street. (Courtesy of Musser Public Library.)

71

MAKING THE FIRST FLAG, MS. SCHMEENK'S CLASS, FOURTH ROOM OF WASHINGTON SCHOOL, 1904. In 1914, *Muscatine of Today* boasted that Muscatine's "school buildings are modern, nine in number, one high school, and eight grammar grades, with four well equipped parochial educational institutions, the standing of which compares most favorably with any other city." (Courtesy of Muscatine Art Center.)

MUSCATINE HIGH SCHOOL (CENTRAL MIDDLE SCHOOL) CHEMISTRY DEPARTMENT, c. 1939. Muscatine's third high school opened in the spring of 1939 at the corner of Ninth and Cedar Streets. The building initially accommodated 750 students in four grade levels and later became home to what is now Central Middle School when the most recent high school building on Cedar Street opened in 1975. (Courtesy of Musser Public Library.)

BELLEVUE HOSPITAL, 1907.
Drs. Arthur J. Weaver
and John L. Klein opened
Bellevue Hospital in 1905 at
205 Cherry Street. Located
on a bluff overlooking
the Mississippi River, the
former private residence
was converted into
operating space and patient
rooms. Nurses initially
lived on the third floor
of the building but were
later housed in a nearby
home purchased by the
hospital board. (Courtesy
of Muscatine Art Center.)

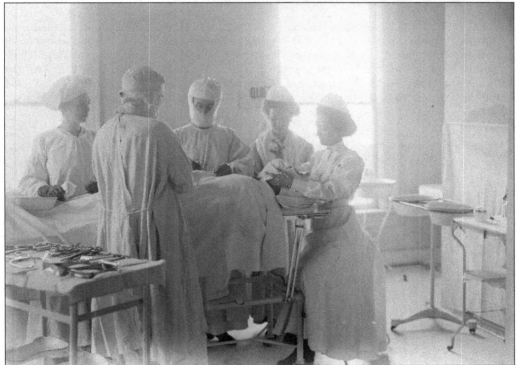

BELLEVUE HOSPITAL SURGICAL PROCEDURE, 1910. A rear addition was added to the hospital in 1940. Bellevue Hospital continued to serve the community until the late 1950s. The building was converted into the Riverview Heights Nursing home in 1960; Riverview Heights closed in 1977. The main building has since been restored into a private residence. (Courtesy of Musser Public Library.)

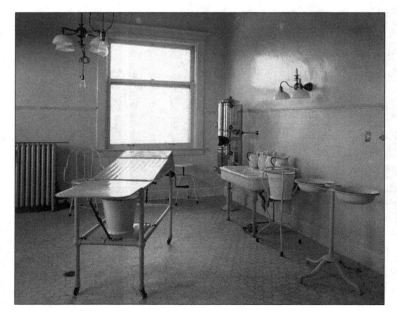

North Mulberry Avenue

Muscatine, Iowa, _Oct 27_____ 191 9

Mr. _W. a. matthews_

To Benjamin Hershey Memorial Hospital Dr.

For Hospital Services Rendered:

Mrs Matthews

From _Oct 18_ 191 9 . to _Oct 25_ 191 9

$ _22.50_

To private room _1_ weeks @ $_17.50_ per week	.	$_17.50_
To bed in Ward........weeks @ $............per week	.	_____
To use of Operating Room	.	_5.00_
To Special Dressing	.	_____
To Drugs	.	_____
To Special Nurse.........weeks @ $............per week	.	_____
To Sp. Nurse Board.........weeks @ $............per week	.	_____
TOTAL	.	_22.50_

Received Payment,

M. Lee McIlwry Superintendent

_E. B._

BENJAMIN HERSHEY MEMORIAL HOSPITAL PAYMENT RECEIPT, 1919. Mira Hershey, daughter of lumber baron Benjamin Hershey, wanted her father's legacy to continue after his death. The Benjamin Hershey Memorial Hospital, located at 1810 Mulberry Avenue, opened in 1902. In 1919, a private room cost $17.50 per week. The private hospital served the community until 1954 when it was converted into a nursing home. (Courtesy of Muscatine Art Center.)

BENJAMIN HERSHEY MEMORIAL HOSPITAL OPERATING ROOM, c. 1902. The main building of the Benjamin Hershey Memorial Hospital was razed in the early 1980s to make way for new senior citizen living quarters. The original nurses' quarters building remains, and the complex known as Hershey Manor is owned and operated by the City of Muscatine. (Courtesy of Musser Public Library.)

Five

MERCHANDIZING PIONEERS

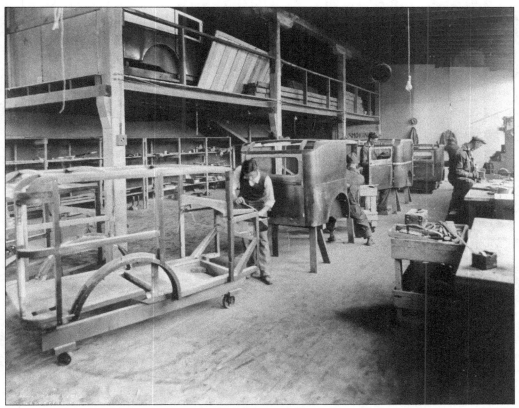

THOMPSON MOTOR CORPORATION, C. 1930. Muscatine County's population swelled to over 28,000 in 1905 on the heels of the booming lumber, button, and agricultural industries. From corner grocery stores to local factories, Muscatine's business districts produced or imported goods and materials for the growing community and several distributed items nationally. Some ventures were short-lived, while others served Muscatine for generations. (Courtesy of Musser Public Library.)

STEIN BLOCK AT SECOND AND PINE STREETS, C. 1870. Simon G. Stein and his cousin Philip Stein founded the S. G. and P. Stein Furniture Company in 1854. The firm, which included a retail operation, was located at the corner of Second and Chestnut Streets. Three years later, the business moved to the corner of Second and Pine Streets. Originally furniture was ordered from Ohio and delivered months later via steamer. Years later, a new store was built across from the Musser Public Library on Iowa Avenue. The S. G. and P. Stein Furniture Company remained in business until 1995. The building was torn down to make way for the current Central State Bank. (Courtesy of Musser Public Library.)

NICHOLAS BARRY, 1900S. Plumbing and heating firm Nicholas Barry and Sons opened in 1870. From its operations at 421 East Second Street, the Barry's installed gas service in homes and businesses throughout Eastern Iowa. The company moved to the corner of Third Street and Mulberry Avenue after it patented a popular lead trap for sinks and washbasins. The business was incorporated as the Barry Manufacturing Company in 1886. (Courtesy of Musser Public Library.)

BARRY COMPANY PULLEY PLANT, 1926. Barry Manufacturing machines revolutionized button manufacturing. The company erected a new plant in 1903 on East Fourth Street near Poplar Street. The facility, which included an iron casting foundry, covered a half-block area. The Barry Pulley Company plant was added nearby in 1915 to manufacture steel pulleys. The same year, the company was incorporated as the Barry Company. (Courtesy of Musser Public Library.)

THE BATTERSON BEE-HIVE, C. 1886. Samuel M. Batterson opened his first Bee-Hive storefront in Wheatland, Iowa, in 1870. His first Muscatine storefront opened in the mid-1880s on the 100 block of West Second Street. By 1891, the business, which started as a general store, had grown into a full-service department store with annual sales of $100,000. The name changed to simply Batterson's after moving to a new location on the 300 block of East Second Street in 1904. Batterson's closed in the 1970s. The Batterson building now houses office and retail space. (Courtesy of Musser Public Library.)

KAUTZ BAKING COMPANY, 1908. German immigrant Michael Kautz opened his bakery at 114 East Third Street in 1874. Soon the Kautz Baking Company would become one of the largest distributors of baked goods in southeast Iowa and western Illinois. The Kautz delivery system, which initially included a fleet of delivery wagons, boasted bread could be delivered "pipin' hot" to Muscatine residences. (Courtesy of Musser Public Library.)

KAUTZ BAKING COMPANY HOLSUM BREAD WRAPPER, C. 1950. The Kautz Baking Company later moved to a three-story brick building on East Third Street (where the Stanley Group offices are now located). This building burned in 1953 and the bakery moved to 207 East Second Street (now Muscatine Computer Store) before closing in 1958. (Courtesy of Muscatine Art Center.)

W. H. STEWART,

MANUFACTURER AND DEALER IN

BOOTS

AND

SHOES,

Keeps constantly on hand a large and general assortment of Eastern *Boots & Shoes of every description*, which he will sell low. Also, a large assortment of his own manufacture. Persons in the trade who will give him a call will find his establishment the place to get an article that will give entire satisfaction.

165 Second Street, sign of Big Black Boot,

MUSCATINE, IOWA.

STEWART NEWSPAPER ADVERTISEMENT, 1860s. In 1854, William Stewart and his son Theodore opened one of the first local boot and shoe stores at 165 Second Street (now 127 East Second Street). A wooden "Big Black Boot" hung outside the store beckoned residents to stop in. Shoes were originally made to order, and in the early years as many as 20 shoemakers worked for Stewart. (Courtesy of Muscatine Art Center.)

WILSON'S SHOE STORE ADVERTISEMENT, 1910s. Irish immigrant John Wilson was 19 years old when he started crafting boots for William Stewart. In 1890, John Wilson and his brother-in-law Tom Cherry purchased the shop, and it was reorganized as Wilson and Cherry. Wilson later became sole owner, and the shop was renamed Wilson's Shoe Store. (Courtesy of Muscatine Art Center.)

WILSON'S SHOE STORE, C. 1938. At one time, Wilson's Show Store was the oldest operating shoe store in Iowa. The business operated out of its original location at 127 East Second Street. It remained in the Wilson family until it closed in 2004. (Courtesy of Musser Public Library.)

KAUFMANN AND SONS CIGAR SHOP ON EAST SECOND STREET, 1886. Cigar manufacturing was a large trade in Muscatine for decades. P. W. Hamilton first started rolling cigars locally in 1842. By 1902, there were 16 cigar makers in Muscatine and at least one cigar box factory. Albert Ekelberg, whose shop was on Lincoln Boulevard, was the last cigar maker in Muscatine. His shop closed in 1946. (Courtesy of Muscatine Art Center.)

BOWMAN LIVERY, C. 1903. Frank Bowman opened a livery and stable in the 1880s, reportedly with two blind horses and one wagon. The barn was located on Front Street (Mississippi Drive) between Sycamore and Cedar Streets. By the dawn of the 20th century, the business had grown to two separate barns and included 150 buggies and carriages, 100 horses, and more than 50 wagons. Families and private business also boarded horses and transportation rigs at Bowman's. (Courtesy of Musser Public Library.)

BENJAMIN LILLY DRY GOODS STORE FIRE, 1916. Muscatine native Benjamin Lilly partnered with N. H. Hine to open a dry goods store at the corner of Second Street and Iowa Avenue in 1881. Fifteen years later, Lilly purchased the business outright. An explosion and fire destroyed the store in 1916, but firefighters were able to keep the blaze from burning through the rest of the downtown area. The business never reopened. (Courtesy of Musser Public Library.)

LAUREL BUILDING CONSTRUCTION, 1917. Months after the Lilly fire, construction on the Laurel Building began on the same site at the corner of Iowa Avenue and Second Street. The six-floor tan brick building was named for Laura Musser, daughter of lumber baron Peter Musser. The Laurel Building remains one of the tallest structures still standing in downtown Muscatine. (Courtesy of Muscatine Art Center.)

LAUREL BUILDING, 1920s. The Laurel Building housed a series of retailers after it opened in 1917. McColm Dry Goods Company was the first, followed by J. C. Penny and later Spurgeon's Retail Mercantile Store. Stanley Consultants purchased the Laurel Building in 1971, and it serves as office space as well as the home of the Stanley Foundation. (Courtesy of Muscatine Art Center.)

McColm Dry Goods Store, 1905. James McColm opened his two-floor dry goods store in 1870 on the 100 block of East Second. The name was changed 20 years later to McColm Dry Goods Company when James's son Edwin joined his father in managing the store. Inventory grew to include apparel, house wares, and window and floor coverings. The store's motto was "Merchandise of proven quality at the lowest possible prices." (Courtesy of Musser Public Library.)

McColm Dry Goods Store Ground Floor, 1918. By 1918, McColm Dry Goods relocated to the first four floors of the newly completed Laurel Building. In 1929, national retailer J. C. Penny moved into the lower two floors of the Laurel Building. McColm Dry Goods continued to sell its wares on the next two floors. Edwin McColm died in 1933; the store closed in 1963 following the death of his wife, Laura Musser McColm Atkins. (Courtesy of Muscatine Art Center.)

MUSCATINE HEINZ PLANT, 1909. Henry J. Heinz personally assessed Muscatine County's agricultural productivity before deciding to open his company's fourth plant in Muscatine. The "pickle works" facility at Isett Avenue and Clay Street opened in 1893, making it the first plant outside of the Heinz Company's headquarters in Pittsburgh, Pennsylvania. Several expansions later, Heinz continues to produce ketchup, soups, and sauces at the same location. (Courtesy of Musser Public Library.)

MUSCATINE OAT MEAL COMPANY, 1890S. In 1879, a group of local businessmen headed by Simon G. Stein started the Muscatine Oat Meal Company. Located at Front (Mississippi Drive) and Pine Streets in the former Bennett's Mill, the company grew to be one of the largest in America on the popularity of its Friends Oats brand. By 1901, the factory could produce 60,000 packages daily. (Courtesy of Muscatine Art Center.)

FRIENDS OATS ADVERTISEMENT, C. 1890. General manager Frank Sawyer's daughter Aura May became the famous young face of Friends Oats, and the cereal's two-pound package propelled the brand's success. The Muscatine Oat Meal Company comprised several buildings, including grain elevators located on the riverside of Front Street (Mississippi Drive). Conveyors transferred grain from storage, and the oats were processed with special cutting machines. (Courtesy of Muscatine Art Center.)

GREAT WESTERN CEREAL COMPANY, C. 1905. Muscatine Oat Meal Company and several other independent mills merged in 1901 to form the Great Western Cereal Company. Frank Sawyer and Simon G. Stein served as directors of the new company, whose products included Mother's Oats. The Quaker Oats Company purchased great Western Cereal in 1911, and Muscatine's cereal production moved to Cedar Rapids, Iowa, a few years later. (Courtesy of Musser Public Library.)

THOMPSON MOTOR CORPORATION, C. 1930. Brothers Herbert and Ralph Thompson organized the Thompson Motor Corporation in 1929 just days before the Wall Street stock market crash that sparked the Great Depression of the 1930s. Both brothers were well-known local attorneys. Ralph was a state senator and Herbert was mayor of Muscatine when the company was founded. (Courtesy of Musser Public Library.)

THOMPSON MOTOR CORPORATION LITTLEMAC ADVERTISING PHOTOGRAPH, C. 1930. Thompson Motor Corporation was founded to produce an automobile coupe called the Littlemac, which was based on a prototype Clayton E. Frederickson built as one of the founders of the short-lived Moline Motor Company in Illinois. Thompson Motor Corporation manufactured from a rented facility at 708 East Fourth Street. (Courtesy of Muscatine Art Center.)

THE LITTLEMAC BROCHURE, 1930. A redesigned coupe debuted at the Chicago Automobile Show. Brochures claimed the Littlemac was "the fastest small automobile in the world," capable of a cruising speed of 55 miles per hour and a fuel economy of 35 miles per gallon. The advertised price was $350. (Courtesy of Muscatine Art Center.)

ROTH OIL LITTLEMAC, C. 1935. Production on a small delivery vehicle, dubbed the "Truckette," began in 1931. The right-hand drive vehicle was designed to make the delivery of small packages quick and efficient. The Kautz Baking Company took delivery of a Truckette in August 1931. This Littlemac, owned by Muscatine's Roth Oil Company, is considered the last one produced. (Courtesy of Muscatine Art Center.)

THOMPSON MOTOR CORPORATION, c. 1930. Although the Littlemac and Truckette were considered solid vehicles, low sales coupled with a lack of investors during the Great Depression spelled the demise of the Thompson Motor Corporation. The company existed on paper in 1935, but actual manufacturing had ceased a few years earlier. (Courtesy of Musser Public Library.)

HOTEL MUSCATINE CONSTRUCTION, c. 1915. As Muscatine continued to prosper, so did the desire for a first-class hotel. In 1914, the Commercial Hotel at the corner of Iowa Avenue and Front Street (Mississippi Drive) was razed to make way for the Hotel Muscatine. Paul Hyland of Chicago, architect of the nearby Muscatine State Bank (now Miller and Harrison Insurance), designed the new establishment. (Courtesy of Musser Public Library.)

Hotel Muscatine Lobby, c. 1915. Completed in 1915, the Hotel Muscatine cost $225,000 to build and featured dozens of sleeping rooms, a stately lobby with velvet furnishings, and dozens of amenities. The hotel remained in operation into the 1990s, although portions of the building had been converted to office, retail, and restaurant space. The remaining hotel rooms were turned into private condominiums by 2008. (Courtesy of Musser Public Library.)

PETER-MAR TOYS SELL THEMSELVES -

There is a reason for the popularity of Peter-Mar Toys—It is a Beautiful, Distinctive, Fast Selling line. Take careful note of the attractive design and finish — you will agree they have EYE APPEAL. Light-weight, doweled and glued, wood construction means . . . . SAFETY APPEAL. Actual tests with children have proved they have

FARM WAGON (removable box)____6⅞ inches high — 19¼ inches long.

unusual . . . . PLAY

Peter-Mar Toys are

Only carefully selecte

by the finish.

TRACTOR ____

Peter Products Company

sales
eye-appeal
play-value
safety-value
) Power!

It's the craftsmanship!

UE. All this adds up to a greater SALES POWER.

ilt by craftsmen with years of wood-working experience.

well-seasoned woods are used — no poor wood is covered

8 inches high — 12 inches long.

MUSCATINE, IOWA

PETER PRODUCTS COMPANY ADVERTISEMENT, C. 1945. In 1941, Ralph Lohr and Clifford Hakes formed the Peter Products Company to manufacture wooden household items for Sears Roebuck and Company. When lumber became scarce during World War II, the men shifted their production to toys. Initially they designed and fashioned military-style jeeps and guns from scrap lumber. Other creations, including farm equipment, followed and were marketed under the name Peter-Mar. At its height, the company employed nearly 50 workers and shipped more than 80 percent of its products to major cities and Eastern states. (Courtesy of Muscatine Art Center.)

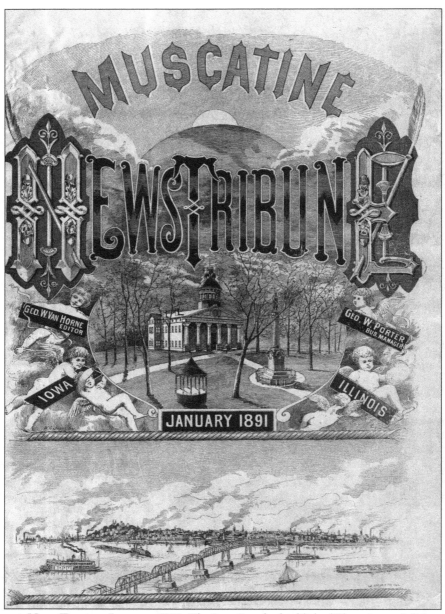

MUSCATINE NEWS TRIBUNE, JANUARY 1891. The *Iowa Standard* published Bloomington's (Muscatine's) first newspaper on October 23, 1840. The following week, The *Bloomington Herald* (later named the *Muscatine Journal*) issued its first edition. Muscatine's first German newspaper, the *Zeitung*, opened in 1857 to serve the town's growing immigrant population. During the next 50 years, multiple newspaper operations including the *Muscatine News Tribune* opened, changed hands, or closed. By 1899, at least six publications supplied news to Muscatine residents on a regular basis. This included the German-language publications *Der Correspondent* and *Deutscher Anzeiger*. In 1903, the longtime *Muscatine Journal* editor John Mahin sold the paper to the Lee Syndicate. The *Muscatine Journal* remains a publication of Lee Enterprises and publishes six editions a week. (Courtesy of Muscatine Art Center.)

Six

PARKS, RECREATION, AND REVIVALS

PARASOL GIRLS PARADA, 1910. Business and industry defined Muscatine's first 100 years, but a wealth of cultural spirit blossomed beyond the factories and fields. Benevolent families generously donated acres of land for city parks, music and theaters entertained the masses, and spiritual events and revivals energized the faithful. (Courtesy of Musser Public Library.)

WEED PARK ENTRANCE, C. 1938. Dr. James and Mary Weed deeded 63 acres of their farm to the City of Muscatine in 1899. The deed cost $1 and required the city to lease the land to the Muscatine Park and Floral Association. The association spearheaded fund drives for park improvements and was the forerunner to the Muscatine Park Commission. (Courtesy of Muscatine Art Center.)

WEED PARK CLUBHOUSE, 1909. The Weed Park Clubhouse, opened in 1906, was a prominent fixture in the park until consumed by fire on June 30, 1930. A group known as the Weed Park Club was instrumental in developing the building. It was primarily used for social events, weddings, and other community activities. The memorial rose garden is located on the site of the former clubhouse. (Courtesy of Musser Public Library.)

WEED PARK SWIMMING POOL, 1921. The Weed Park swimming pool was dedicated on August 21, 1921. The pool cost $20,000 to construct. It measured 50 feet by 100 feet and included a bathhouse. Admission in 1921 was free, but initially women were only allowed to use the facility on Thursdays. The pool's popularity grew quickly with 35,000 swimmers using it in 1923. (Courtesy of Musser Public Library.)

WEED PARK LIFEGUARDS, 1920s. The pool was rededicated in 1949 after an extensive remodeling project. The bathhouse was renovated in 1980. The pool closed in 2002 and was replaced in 2004 by the modern Muscatine Aquatic Center, which was built in an adjacent field. The original Weed Park pool was later filled in and the bathhouse dismantled. (Courtesy of Muscatine Art Center.)

DOLLY THE ELEPHANT AT WEED PARK ZOO, 1965. The Weed Park Zoo started with the donation of two honey bears in 1921. It featured hundreds of animals over the years, including an elephant named Dolly, tigers, antelope, peacocks, monkeys, and reptiles. The Muscatine City Council voted in 1980 to sell the animals and close the facility. Dolly and other animal favorites are now memorialized as statues in the Weed Park Zoo Garden. (Courtesy of Musser Public Library.)

CITIZENS ELECTRIC PARK, 1907. The Citizens Railway Park opened on May 30, 1903. It was located at Bidwell Road and Park Lane. Complete with strings of lights, the 18-acre grounds originally included a dancing pavilion and dining hall. Summer activities included theatre, band concerts, and bowling. (Courtesy of Musser Public Library.)

CHAUTAUQUA CAMO UNO, CITIZENS ELECTRIC PARK, C. 1907. Citizens Electric Park was the early home of the local Chautauqua movement. During the popular summer education event, the park would transform into a tent city of families and businesses. In 1907, William Jennings Bryan spoke to a crowd of over 7,000 at the Muscatine Chautauqua. (Courtesy of Musser Public Library.)

MUSSER PARK PATHWAY, 1921. In 1919, Peter Miller Musser donated 10 acres of the former Musser Lumber Company site on Oregon Street to the City of Muscatine for a public park. The park featured a wood pergola and shelter, which were constructed on the levee. Thanks to an additional cash donation from Musser, walkways, drinking fountains, and restrooms were also added. (Courtesy of Muscatine Art Center.)

MUSSER PARK SHELTER, 1921. A concrete wading pool and skating rink was added in 1926 after a donation from Musser's son Clifton M. Musser. The park continued to evolve with the addition of a baseball diamond and tennis courts. In 2003, the Muscatine Skate Park was added for skateboarding and BMX bike enthusiasts. (Courtesy of Musser Public Library.)

RIVERSIDE PARK, 1933. Located along the shore of the Mississippi River, Riverside Park originally stretched from Cedar Street to Walnut Street. The Muscatine Levee Commission, organized by the city council in 1915, was instrumental in the development of the park. One of the commission's first major projects was the construction of a warehouse and a steamboat landing. (Courtesy of Musser Public Library.)

RIVERSIDE PARK, C. 1930. With a view of the High Bridge, Riverside Park grew into a lush green space complete with trees, shrubs, and flowers. The Muscatine Levee Commission worked with local clubs and fraternal organizations to add a pergola, statues, and a fountain. Many of the early improvements are no longer standing. (Courtesy of Muscatine Art Center.)

VIEW OF RIVERSIDE PARK FROM HIGH BRIDGE, C. 1933. An act of Congress added the portion of land between Orange Street and Mad Creek to Riverside Park in the 1960s. Millions of dollars of improvements have been made since 1990, including Erik Blome's bronze sculpture *Mississippi Harvest* near the park's Iowa Avenue entrance and Millennium Plaza, located near the spot believed to be the site of Casey's Landing. (Courtesy of Muscatine Art Center.)

LEAGUE PARK OPENING DAY, 1910. Muscatine's professional baseball team inaugurated League Park in May 1910. To the delight of fans, the home team won the opening game. On June 12, 1913, a total of 3,600 fans watched the local "Muskies" beat the famed Chicago Cubs. The diamond is now known as Tom Bruner Field and is part of the Kent-Stein Park. (Courtesy of Muscatine Art Center.)

THE GREENWOOD CEMETERY CHAPEL, C. 1905. Lumber baron Peter Musser built the chapel at the city-owned Greenwood Cemetery in memory of his wife, Tamson. It was dedicated in May 1901. Located at the Lucas Street entrance, the building housed the chapel, caretaker apartments, and a depository for incoming burials. The chapel was placed on the National Register of Historic Places in 2001. (Courtesy of Musser Public Library.)

STEIN MUSIC HALL, C. 1900. Simon G. Stein and S. G. Hill constructed Tremont Hall on the 100 block of East Second Street in 1852. Later named Stein Music Hall, it was used for public theatre performances, lectures, and events. The building later housed the McColm Dry Goods Company. Stein Music Hall was torn down in 1953 to make room for a new Woolworth Store. (Courtesy of Musser Public Library.)

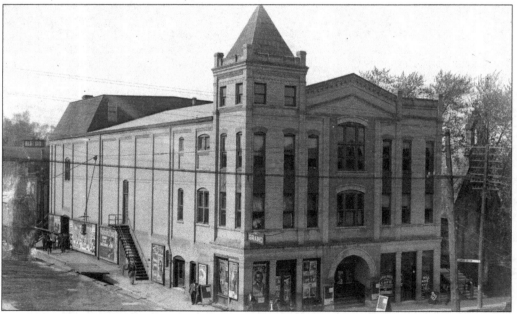

GRAND OPERA HOUSE, C. 1905. The Grand Opera House opened in 1900 at the corner of Second and Walnut Streets adjacent to Trinity Episcopal Church. The facility featured eight private boxes and could seat up to 1,500. The *Muscatine Journal* reported workers installed 7,000 feet of electrical wire for lighting. Later known as the Grand Theater, the building was destroyed by fire in 1945. (Courtesy of Musser Public Library.)

TURNER OPERA HOUSE PERFORMANCE, C. 1885. The Turner Opera House opened in December 1885 with a performance of *Galatea*. The hall, located at Sixth Street and Iowa Avenue, featured gabled cornices, three entrances, and a janitor residence. In 1895, its name was changed to Columbia Opera House. Fire ravaged the building on December 3, 1896. (Courtesy of Musser Public Library.)

PALACE THEATER INTERIOR, 1925. Several theaters continued to entertain the masses after the beginning of the 20th century. In addition to the Grand Theater, performance stages and motion picture screens included the Family Theater (later the Orpheum) on East Third Street, the Palace Theater at 212 Sycamore Street, the A-Muse-U Theater at 105 Sycamore Street, and the Crystal Theater at 303 East Second Street. (Courtesy of Musser Public Library.)

YMCA Indoor Pool, 1917. Construction on the YMCA building at the corner of Fourth Street and Iowa Avenue commenced in 1902. The blueprints did not include a swimming pool; however, Peter Miller Musser later donated money for the pool. The facility was replaced in the 1950s with the building that now houses the Muscatine Center for Social Action (MCSA). "Rest rooms" established for women visiting Muscatine led to the creation of the local YWCA in 1905. First housed on upper floors of the Stein Building on East Second Street, the initial membership fee was $1. A new facility at 305 Sycamore was dedicated in 1924. Fire gutted the building in 1987, and it was torn down to make way for a city parking lot. (Courtesy of Musser Public Library.)

Seven

INFLUENTIAL RESIDENTS

MARK TWAIN CIGAR BOX, C. 1910. Muscatine produced scores of influential citizens in its first 100 years. Entrepreneurs transformed the local economy, generously invested in the community, and left a legacy of the work ethic that defines the Midwest. Others gained international fame, promoted controversial cancer cures, and pioneered Iowa's civil rights movement. All of these people contributed to Muscatine's unique story. (Courtesy of Muscatine Art Center.)

SAMUEL CLEMENS, AGE 18.
Aspiring writer Samuel Clemens was 18 years old when he moved to Muscatine. Local lore has Clemens working alongside his brother Orion, then co-owner and editor of the *Muscatine Journal*. It is difficult to pinpoint the exact time Clemens lived in Muscatine. Nine letters penned during his travels away from Muscatine were published in the *Journal* between November 1853 and March 1855. (Courtesy of Musser Public Library.)

CLEMENS HOUSE PHOTOGRAPH, 1930S.
The young Samuel Clemens lived with his family in this rented house at Walnut and Front (Mississippi Drive) Streets. Under the pen name Mark Twain, he later wrote in *Life on the Mississippi*, "I remember Muscatine . . . for its summer sunsets. I have never seen any, on either side of the ocean that equaled them." (Courtesy of Musser Public Library.)

Pigs is Pigs by Ellis Parker Butler, c. 1906. Mark Twain was not the only humorist with local ties. Muscatine native Ellis Parker Butler's 1906 book *Pigs is Pigs* catapulted him to national fame. Featuring character Mike Flannery, the 25¢ publication sold a million copies. Butler drew inspiration for his fictional characters from his youth and work experiences. He quit high school at age 17 and worked odd jobs in Muscatine before moving to New York in 1897. Butler authored more than 30 stories, including *Perkins of Portland*, *That Pup of Murchison's*, and *The Great American Pie Company*, before his death in 1937. (Courtesy of Muscatine Art Center.)

WEST AND THIRD STREETS, 1870s. Alexander Clark settled in Muscatine at age 16. He worked as a barber but also amassed considerable wealth in real estate and selling firewood to passing steamboats. His son Alexander Jr. was the first black graduate of the University of Iowa Law School in 1879. Alexander Sr. followed in his son's footsteps, becoming the second black graduate of the law school in 1884. (Courtesy of Muscatine Art Center.)

ALEXANDER CLARK'S WOOD-FRAME HOUSE, 1870s. Alexander Clark lived at the corner of West Third and Chestnut Streets. The wood-frame home burned in 1878, possibly at the hands of an arsonist. A brick home rose from the ruins. It was moved in 1975 to the 200 block of West Third Street to make way for the multistory Clark House, a publicly subsidized apartment building for senior citizens. (Courtesy of Musser Public Library.)

Court Notice Filed on Behalf of Susan Clark, 1867. In 1867, Clark sued the Muscatine Board of Education after his daughter Susan was not allowed to attend an all-white school. The Iowa Supreme Court sided with Clark. The victory effectively desegregated Iowa schools more than 85 years before the United States Supreme Court ruling *Brown vs. Board of Education* declared racial segregation violated the 14th amendment to the U.S. Constitution. (Courtesy of Muscatine Art Center.)

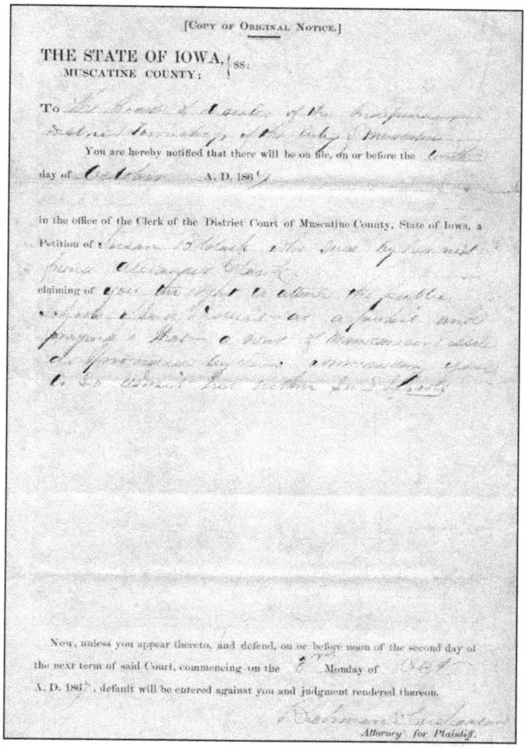

[Copy of Original Notice.]

THE STATE OF IOWA, } ss:
MUSCATINE COUNTY: }

To [illegible]

You are hereby notified that there will be on file, on or before the [illegible] day of October A. D. 1867

in the office of the Clerk of the District Court of Muscatine County, State of Iowa, a Petition of Susan B. Clark who sues by her next friend Alexander Clark

claiming of you the right to attend the public schools [illegible] and praying that a writ of Mandamus issue [illegible]

Now, unless you appear thereto, and defend, on or before noon of the second day of the next term of said Court, commencing on the [illegible] Monday of Oct A. D. 1867, default will be entered against you and judgment rendered thereon.

[illegible]
Attorney for Plaintiff.

DEPARTMENT OF STATE
SEP 2 1890
RECEIVED

I hereby authorize and direct the Secretary of State to cause the Seal of the United States to be affixed to the envelopes covering my letters to the President of Liberia recalling Mr E. E. Smith and accrediting Mr Alexander Clark as Minister Resident & Consul General of the U.S. to Liberia

dated this day, and signed by me, and for so doing this shall be his warrant.

Benj Harrison

Washington, Sept 2 1890

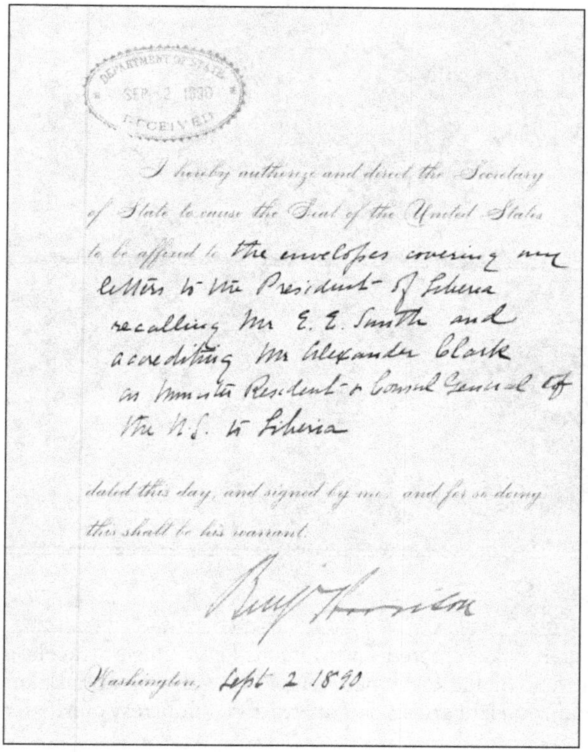

Pres. Benjamin Harrison Letter Regarding Alexander Clark, 1890. Pres. Benjamin Harrison formally appointed Clark minister and consul-general to the West African nation of Liberia with this letter on September 2, 1890. Clark died in Liberia on May 31, 1891, and was later buried in Muscatine's Greenwood Cemetery. (Courtesy of Muscatine Art Center.)

NORMAN BAKER, 1920s. Norman Baker, born locally in 1882, was a flamboyant and controversial resident. His father, John, operated the first boiler factory in Muscatine. Norman quit high school and briefly worked in regional machine shops before joining vaudeville. Later in life, Baker pioneered Muscatine radio and promoted a questionable cancer "cure." (Courtesy of Muscatine Art Center.)

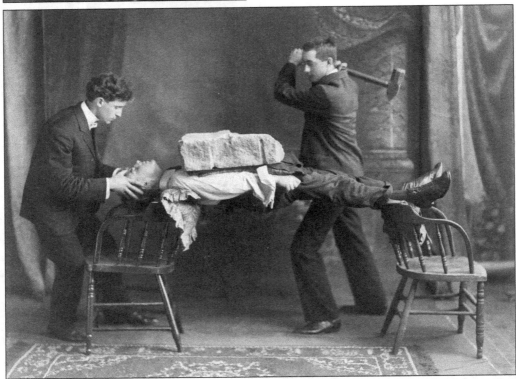

HYPNOSIS DEMONSTRATION, C. 1900. Norman Baker created *The Madame Pearl Tangley* traveling show, claiming his muse could "read the minds" of audience members. In this photograph, Baker is holding the head of an unidentified man during a hypnosis demonstration. (Courtesy of Musser Public Library.)

TANGLEY CALLIAPHONE, 1916. Norman Baker returned to Muscatine in 1914 and opened a calliaphone factory on Front Street (Mississippi Drive). Baker invented and patented the calliaphone, an air-powered version of the circus staple calliope. Fire gutted the factory in 1920, but Baker rebuilt the operation. The calliaphone would become a centerpiece of Baker's radio station. (Courtesy of Muscatine Art Center.)

KTNT CROWD, C. 1930. Norman Baker started Muscatine's first radio station in 1925. Located on the bluff above East Second Street (now known as Mark Twain Overlook), the station's call letters "KTNT" stood for "Know The Naked Truth." The AM station was initially licensed to operate at 500 watts. Baker used the station as an outlet to promote his business ventures and to attack his critics. (Courtesy of Muscatine Art Center.)

KTNT STATION, C. 1928. KTNT was in operation before the establishment of the Federal Radio Commission (FRC), which was the government agency organized in 1927 to govern America's airwaves. As his popularity grew, Baker increased the strength of the station's transmitter. Broadcasts could be heard as far away as Manitoba, Canada, and Hawaii. Citing a growing list of complaints, the FRC refused to renew Baker's license in 1931. The station went dark the same year. (Courtesy of Muscatine Art Center.)

KTNT GAS STATION, C. 1930. Norman Baker, always seeking new entrepreneurial opportunities, expanded his KTNT franchise to include the downtown KTNT restaurant and the KTNT oil company on Second Street near Mad Creek. Baker proclaimed the gas station sold "pure gum rubber tires . . . guaranteed for 16,500 miles." (Courtesy of Muscatine Art Center.)

TANGLEY CIGAR BOX LID, C. 1928. Norman Baker crafted the merchandizing and manufacturing empire Tangley Enterprises. Tangley sold a long list of products, including gum, coffee, paint, batteries, and, of course, radios. Baker sold "Tangley Association Memberships" and boasted he personally oversaw the production of each product. However, most goods were actually made elsewhere and shipped to Muscatine for final labeling. (Courtesy of Muscatine Art Center.)

TNT MAGAZINE, 1930. Norman Baker supplemented his radio station broadcasts with print publications. For $2 a year, readers could subscribe to the print magazine *TNT*. Baker's own short-lived newspaper, *The Midwest Free Press*, began publication in 1930 from offices located at 408 East Second Street. (Courtesy of Muscatine Art Center.)

Baker Hospital Photograph, 1935. The Baker Muscatine Cancer Hospital opened in November 1929 with the slogan, "Cancer is Curable." The hospital, which Norman Baker later called an "institute," was located at 405 East Front Street (Mississippi Drive). Baker organized public events to demonstrate his "cure." Baker admitted in the 1930s he did not have formal medical training. (Courtesy of Muscatine Art Center.)

KTNT Weed Park Mass Meeting, 1930. Over 17,000 people were reportedly on hand to witness Norman Baker's medical team partially remove the scalp and skull of Mandus Johnson in May 1930. Doctors then administered the cancer "treatment," and Baker pronounced Johnson cured. The Baker Institute attracted hundreds of patients, but state and federal medical organizations, including the American Medical Association, quickly questioned the cancer "cure." (Courtesy of Muscatine Art Center.)

116

LETTER OF INQUIRY TO MUSCATINE CHAMBER OF COMMERCE, 1935.

The American Medical Association denounced the cancer "quackery," and Norman Baker sued the organization for libel. Baker lost the suit in 1932. The same year, Baker built a radio station in Nuevo Laredo, Mexico. Continued scrutiny and the threat of legal action eventually forced Baker to leave Muscatine altogether. He returned in 1936 to campaign during the final months of his failed gubernatorial bid. In 1937, Baker moved his cancer institute to the Ozarks. In this letter, Mrs. O. M. Paddock of Kansas seeks validation from the chamber of commerce regarding Baker's cancer hospital. "Do you think he is as reliable as his advertisement over the air sound?" she writes. (Courtesy of Muscatine Art Center.)

Mound City, Kansas
March 4, 1935

Chamber of Commerce
    Muscatine, Iowa
Gentlemen:

I am writing this to see if you would give me some information in regard to the Dr. Baker hospital and his work there in Muscatine.

Do you think he is as reliable as his advertisment over the air sound?

I have a relative who is in a very serious condition and the Doctors here say they can do nothing for him, so we would like very much to have your opinion of this Dr. Baker.

Thanking you very much I remain

Yours Very Truly

Mrs. O. M. Paddock

R F D No. 1

Mound City, Kansas

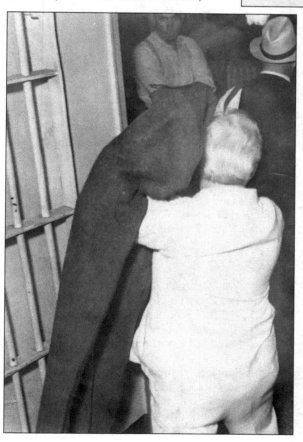

NORMAN BAKER AT THE MUSCATINE COUNTY JAIL, 1936.

In 1936, Norman Baker spent one night in the Muscatine County Jail for practicing medicine without a license. He was convicted of mail fraud in 1940 and served time in the Leavenworth Federal Penitentiary. Baker moved to Florida after his release and died there in 1958. He is buried in Muscatine's Greenwood Cemetery. (Courtesy of Muscatine Art Center.)

TRINITY EPISCOPAL CHURCH, 1908. Josiah Proctor Walton, an 1838 settler, briefly farmed on the Muscatine Island and was instrumental in the construction of the county's early levee system. Walton later designed many homes and buildings including Trinity Episcopal Church and "The Gables," the home built for Dr. James Weed that is still located on Oakland Drive. Walton also recorded local weather observations for more than 30 years. (Courtesy of Musser Public Library.)

IRVING RICHMAN, 1910s. Attorney Irving B. Richman represented Muscatine in the Iowa Legislature in the late 1880s and early 1890s. He authored two volumes of Muscatine County history in 1911. The work remains one of the most comprehensive reviews of local history, although the effort borrows heavily from earlier publications and contains many inaccuracies. (Courtesy of Muscatine Art Center.)

GROSSHEIM BROTHERS, 1880s. Oscar Grossheim's photography career began in 1877 with an apprenticeship at the age of 15. Grossheim developed a portable camera in the 1880s. The invention was not mass-produced, although the camera attracted the attention of George Eastman of the Eastman-Kodak Company. Oscar and his older brother Alexander opened their own studio in 1886. (Courtesy of Muscatine Art Center.)

OSCAR GROSSHEIM STOREFRONT AT NIGHT, c. 1940. Oscar Grossheim ended the partnership with his brother in 1892 and opened a studio at 317 East Second Street, now Wester Drug Store. He earned national awards for his portraits. His work was also included in *The Traveling Loan Collections of the Photographers Association of America*. (Courtesy of Musser Public Library.)

OSCAR GROSSHEIM IN STUDIO, 1920S. Oscar Grossheim's portfolio included individual and family portraits, businesses and street scenes, product advertisements, and obituary photographs. By the time of his death in 1954, Grossheim had amassed more than 55,000 images of Muscatine and the surrounding region. The glass-plate negatives, many of which were nearly thrown out after his death, are now housed at the Musser Public Library. (Courtesy of Muscatine Art Center.)

MUSCATINE GRANGE FACTORY AT THIRD STREET AND MULBERRY AVENUE, C. 1875. Oliver Hudson Kelley is considered the "father" of the Order of the Patrons of Husbandry, also known as the Grange. The Boston-born Kelly moved to Bloomington (Muscatine) in 1848 and served briefly as a telegraph operator before moving to Minnesota and later Washington, D.C., where he and others formed the fraternal farm organization in 1867. (Courtesy of Musser Public Library.)

SUEL FOSTER, 1870S. Horticultural pioneer Suel Foster was one of Muscatine County's earliest settlers. The New Hampshire native moved to the area in 1836. Foster served on the first board of trustees for the Iowa Agricultural College, established in 1848. The college was built in Ames and later became Iowa State University. Foster also owned Muscatine's Foster Hill Nursery. He died in 1886. (Courtesy of Musser Public Library.)

JOHN MAHIN, C. 1902. Indiana native John Mahin started working for the *Bloomington Herald* at age 13. The *Herald* was renamed the *Muscatine Journal* in 1849. In 1852, Mahin became publisher at the age of 19. Mahin divested the paper in 1854 but repurchased an interest two years later. The *Muscatine Journal* published from a number of locations in its early years before planting roots on what is now the 200 block of Iowa Avenue in 1861. The newspaper moved to its current location at the corner of East Third and Cedar Streets in 1919. Mahin served as editor for half a century until his retirement in 1903. That year, the *Muscatine Journal* became part of the Lee Syndicate, a company started by Alfred Lee, the brother of Mahin's wife. The *Muscatine Journal* remains a publication of Lee Enterprises and publishes six editions a week. (Courtesy of Muscatine Art Center.)

JOHN MAHIN SITTING ROOM BOMB DAMAGE, 1893. John Mahin served as Muscatine's postmaster from 1861 to 1869 and again from 1873 to 1878. He was elected to the Iowa House of Representatives in 1869 and served for two years. He was a passionate supporter of the Union during the Civil War, and later he served as secretary of the Soldiers Monument Association, which was instrumental in raising the courthouse Civil War monument. Mahin was a vocal opponent of Muscatine's saloons. Opponents of his campaign for prohibition turned violent on May 11, 1893. Mahin's home at 513 West Second Street was firebombed, as were the homes of businessman Elias M. Kessinger and attorney Nathan Rosenberger. Thankfully no one was seriously injured. Resident Mort Woods was later convicted of the crimes. Mahin sold the *Muscatine Journal* in 1903 and retired to Evanston, Illinois. He died there on July 24, 1919, and is buried in Muscatine's Greenwood Cemetery. (Courtesy of Musser Public Library.)

LAURA MUSSER, C. 1900. Laura Musser was born in Muscatine in 1877 to Peter C. and Tamson Rhodes Musser. In 1903, Laura married Edwin L. McColm, the president and owner of Muscatine's leading dry goods store. The couple and Laura's father moved to a new home at 1314 Mulberry Avenue five years later. A trained vocalist, Laura Musser McColm was awarded an honorary doctorate in music from Iowa Wesleyan College. She later served on the college's board of trustees. Edwin McColm died in 1933. Laura married William T. Atkins in 1938 and relocated to Kansas City, Missouri. (Courtesy of Muscatine Art Center.)

LAURA MUSSER MANSION, 1910. Muscatine native Henry W. Zeidler designed the Laura Musser McColm mansion in the Edwardian style. A total of 12 rooms flank the central hall, and the home is decorated and adorned with period details. The music room was added in 1921 to accommodate an Etsey Player pipe organ. After her marriage to William Atkins and her subsequent move to Missouri, Laura frequently visited Muscatine and retained ownership of the home until her death in 1964. A year later her heirs, stepdaughter Mary Catherine McWhirter and niece Mary Musser Gilmore, donated the home and grounds to the city in her memory. It now comprises a portion of the Muscatine Art Center. (Courtesy of Muscatine Art Center.)

BIBLIOGRAPHY

Alexander, Melanie K. *Muscatine's Pearl Button Industry*. Charleston, SC: Arcadia Publishing, 2007.

Bekker, Marilyn A. *Heritage Vignettes*. Muscatine, IA: Muscatine Area Heritage Association, 1976.

Carlson, Jon. *Muscatine, A Pictorial History*. Rock Island, IL: Quest Publishing, 1984.

encyclopedia.chicagohistory.org

History of Muscatine County, Iowa. Chicago: Chicago Western Historical Society, 1879.

iagenweb.org/muscatine

Jackson, Marilyn. "From Rafts to Riches, the Story of Muscatine's Lumber Barons." *The Iowan*: Spring, 1983.

Jepsen, Bill, *Iowa's Automobiles: Made in Iowa: An Entertaining and Enlightening History*. Self-published, 2007.

Juhnke, Eric, *Quacks and Crusaders: The Fabulous Careers of John Brinkley, Norman Baker, and Harry Hoxsey*. Lawrence, KS: University Press of Kansas, 2002.

Lewis, H. W. *Picturesque Muscatine*. Davenport, IA: The Democrat Company Printers, 1901.

Muscatine City Directory, various editions from 1856–1959.

Muscatine of Today. Muscatine, IA: Home Record Printing Company, 1914.

Muscatine Journal, various editions including the Semi-Centennial Souvenir, 1891; The Centennial Souvenir, June 24, 1933; Centennial Edition, May 21, 1940; Bicentennial Edition, July 1, 1976; Sesquicentennial Edition, August 12, 1983.

Petersen, William J. "Beginnings of Muscatine." *Palimpsest* 45, no. 9 (1964).

pinecreekgristmill.com

Randleman, Douglas. *Greetings from Muscatine, A Pictorial Postcard History*. Muscatine, IA: Knott Printers, Inc., 1981.

Richman, Irving. *History of Muscatine County, Iowa*. Chicago: S.J. Clark Publishing Company, 1911.

Walton, Josiah Proctor. *Pioneer Papers*, Muscatine, IA: 1899.

www.co.muscatine.ia.us/community/his.shtml

Visit us at
arcadiapublishing.com